So you want to be
a librarian…

So you want to be
a librarian…

By Lauren Pressley

Library Juice Press
Duluth, Minnesota

Copyright Lauren Pressley, 2008

Published in 2009

Published by Library Juice Press
P.O. Box 3320
Duluth, MN 55803
http://libraryjuicepress.com/

Library of Congress Cataloging-in-Publication Data

Pressley, Lauren.
 So you want to be a librarian! / by Lauren Pressley.
     p. cm.
 Summary: "Provides information about librarianship as a ca-
reer, including types of libraries, types of jobs within libraries,
professional issues, and educational requirements"--Provided
by publisher.
 Includes bibliographical references and index.
 ISBN 978-0-9802004-8-5 (acid-free paper)
1. Library science--Vocational guidance. 2. Library science--
Vocational guidance--United States. I. Title.
 Z682.35.V62P74 2009
 020.7--dc22
                                        2009009516

To Grace James, the librarian who introduced me to this wonderful type of work while I was just an elementary school student. I still think fondly of volunteering at your library during the summers, of reading as many books as I possibly could, of riding in your red convertible with the unbelievably fun license plate, and of lunches at the Pavilion. It is because of your work that I have loved libraries for as long as I can remember.

Acknowledgments

Librarianship is a field of helpful people. While writing this book I have had the opportunity to engage in several informative conversations about the profession with a number of interesting librarians. This book is better for it. Thank you to Kathleen Burlingame, Mary Chimato, Ellie Collier, Kim Duckett, Audra Eagle, Amy Kearns, Sue Kimmel, Cliff Landis, Cat McDowell, Melissa Rethlefsen, Courtney Stephens, and Rachel Walden for taking the time to share their perspectives on the profession. This book represents a broader view of the field because of your contributions.

Thank you to Lauren Corbett, Jenny McCraw Dale, Craig Fansler, Stephen Francoeur, Jim Galbraith, Kate Kapetanakis, Steve Kelley, Brian Mathews, Carolyn McCallum, David Rothman, Anna Van Scoyoc, Jason Setzer, Sarah Rothstein Smith, Sharon Snow, Courtney Stephens, Brandi Tuttle, and Joe Williams for helping me understand the various facets of the field and for looking at different parts of this text. This book is clearer and more accurate for it.

Lynn Sutton and Susan Smith are remarkable mentors, and I thank them for helping me find my place in the profession and for their good advice for a new writer. Thank you to Mary Horton and Erik Mitchell, who have been supportive and encouraging supervisors throughout this process. Thank you to Mary Lib Slate, Kaeley McMahan, Kevin Gilbertson, Elizabeth Novicki, Mary Scanlon, and Sarah Jeong for the conversations along the way. And thank you to Rosalind Tedford, Giz Womack, Ellen Daugman,

Bobbie Collins, and Tim Mitchell, for being such supportive colleagues.

I would especially like to thank Rory Litwin and Library Juice Press for giving me a chance to do something so exciting so early in my career and for giving me the opportunity to gain a fuller perspective on the profession.

Thank you to all of my family for your interest, support, and forgone weekends to ensure I finished this project. And finally, to the one who was most aware of just how intense this project was: thanks to my amazingly supportive husband, John Borwick, who encourages me to be the best I can be, while helping me stay calm and balanced. This book is better for it, and so am I.

Contents

Introduction

The choice of a career is an important one. We spend most of our conscious hours at our jobs, and the tone of our workdays can influence our personal lives. Many of us derive a sense of purpose from the mission of our careers, and we spend a lifetime building a body of work. Because of the importance of career in our lives, many of us want to find a career that is ethically suitable, interesting, and meaningful. Most of us would also like a career that challenges us to experiment and continue learning, and one that gives us the opportunity to work with interesting people.

Happily, there is librarianship, a career that meets all of these requirements. Librarianship, as a field, is grounded in its professional ethics and values. Librarians have the opportunity to learn something new and help other people every day, just by the virtue of their job descriptions. As technology changes how people access information, librarians experiment with new services, formats, and ways of doing business. Creativity and innovation are rewarded and valued by the profession. Such an appealing field draws interesting people as well, either as a first career or one chosen later in life.

The goal of this book is to help you decide if librarianship might be the career for you, whether you are just graduating college or are switching careers later in life. This book provides a basic overview of the profession so that no matter your current situation, you can gain a basic understanding of the field, the types of jobs available, trends, and the paths to getting professional employment.

Some challenges are unique to those graduating from school. For those just coming from college, your search for post-college work or education is the first time you must confront how to make a living. Where should you live? Where should you work? What could you study? From kindergarten through college, each step of life has clearly led to the next: elementary school to middle school, and high school to college. You will now have more independence in and responsibility for what you do—ultimately, you must figure out what career path to pursue.

Librarianship appeals to many students because the profession values the academic background that you have worked so hard to gain. You may even get to purchase books in your area of expertise if you work in an academic or public library. Any college major can be useful in a library setting. It is in a library's best interest to have a number of librarians who specialize in different subjects. This allows the library to address a broad range of fields. A library with a wide spectrum of subject experts can provide service for patrons with complex questions; someone can answer the question, no matter the discipline.

People switching careers face challenges as well. You might have been out of school for some time and prefer not to return. It can be a difficult decision to leave a mid-level or management position to take an entry-level position in a new field. Inevitably, changing careers means losing expert status in your current field, and becoming a novice in another one.

However, those coming to the field from other professions bring strengths as well. For example, with industry expertise, you are prepared to work in libraries within your former industry. You are also prepared to help students studying to join your former industry. Some professions have skill sets that are useful to librarianship. For example, a previous career in marketing can provide useful skills that many libraries might be looking to add to their staff. The same could be true for computer programming, the legal field, communications, and a host of other careers.

Whether you are about to graduate from college or you have worked in another profession for a number of years, librarianship could be the career for you. Librarians often refer to librarianship as a last haven for generalists. Make no mistake: librarians are experts in their subject areas. However, to excel, a librarian ought to know something about many other fields. Even if you are a specialist in one discipline, you have the opportunity to work with people interested in any subject area the library supports, and you should know enough to help with the most basic requests. Whether you sit at a reference desk or catalog materials, at some point you could make use of anything you have ever learned!

Whether you majored in the liberal arts, sciences, or business, or whether you have spent the last fifteen years doing something that seems entirely unrelated, you might find librarianship one of the most exciting fields open to you today. If you enjoy research, information, education, how people communicate, or the Internet, librarianship offers exciting and innovative work opportunities. If you have ideas about the future of libraries and research, this is an excellent time to join the profession. Both librarians and the mainstream media debate the place of libraries in the future, so the profession is facing a period of redefinition. If you have good ideas and want to contribute to the conversation, your voice will be heard.

Librarianship is also a profession that is built on an ethical foundation. The profession has its own Library Bill of

Rights[1] and Code of Ethics.[2] Community, rather than profit, motivates librarians. At the end of a workday, most librarians have helped people or made a positive impact on their community. We do not measure success in revenue but whether the library meets the needs of the users.[3] A librarian's work may include marketing, but the marketing aims to let the community know about services that exist to genuinely help people.

Librarianship also appeals to people who like learning. If you like academia, or have specialized in a subject without an obvious career path, you can find a home in librarianship. If you are the type of person who loves school, you will love librarianship. Librarians do have to earn an ALA[4] accredited master's degree, which this book will discuss in detail in chapter five. Some librarians also earn an additional master's degree in their subject area of choice. Librarianship can give you an excuse, or a justification, to get the MA in

---

[1] The Library Bill of Rights can be found at
http://www.ala.org/ala/aboutala/offices/oif/statementspols/statementsif/librarybillrights.cfm
[2] The Code of Ethics for the American Library Association can be found at
http://www.ala.org/ala/aboutala/offices/oif/statementspols/codeofethics/codeethics.cfm
[3] "Meet the needs of the users!" was the mantra of one of my library school professors, Dr. Bea Kovacs.
[4] ALA stands for American Library Association. The American Library Association certifies graduate programs, holds conferences, and is the major professional organization for librarians in the United States. (Canadian librarians have their own organization, the Canadian Library Association, but are often members of ALA as well.) The abbreviation "ALA" will be used throughout this book in place of the full name.

history or musicology that you have always wanted. If, on the other hand, you are tired of school but tempted by library work, you can find interesting and meaningful positions in libraries that are not professional librarian positions. If you change your mind in the future, you can pursue the ALA accredited degree at that time.

Librarianship appeals to people because of the nature of the work, as well. If you like helping people, delving into challenging research questions, trivia, using the Internet skillfully, working with students, or teaching, you will likely find something to love in librarianship. If you are service-minded, this field gives you a chance to see a positive difference in your community resulting from your work. If you like focusing on detail-oriented tasks and enjoy organization, there are jobs for you in libraries. If you like to think about the big picture and in abstract and theoretical ways, some positions within librarianship use those skills as well. A shy person can find positions within libraries in which he or she do not interact much with the public. If you like talking with people and presenting, you can find those jobs, too.

And for some people, one of the most exciting aspects of the field is that it is changing. Some suggest that the Internet threatens the existence of libraries. They argue that with the Internet so readily available, there is no need for taxes to fund local libraries. However, libraries continue to exist in most communities and, in fact, offer access to the Internet for users who cannot get access on their own. In this day of technology and change, libraries and librarians seek out new ways to define themselves while maintaining the values and skills that have characterized the field so far. New and young librarians are finding ways to contribute to the larger professional conversation through blogs and other communication technologies. Librarians readily share ideas and successes from individual libraries in an effort to make the profession as a whole a stronger one. Though the future of libraries is unclear, we do know that interested, motivated, and energetic voices help shape its conversation and direction.

About This Book

There are many varied paths that lead to librarianship. In retrospect, I realize I was probably always going to be a librarian. Yet, I did not realize it until after I had graduated from college. I finished my undergraduate degrees with coursework that challenged me intellectually, though it did not have obvious value for the workforce. I had experience from part-time work I did throughout college, but it was not enough to get a job upon graduation. I thought about pursuing a doctoral degree, but with such broad interests I could not narrow my area of study sufficiently for an intensely focused PhD program to make sense. I applied for any job even remotely related to my experiences, and, luckily, ended up with a job that I enjoyed.

That job was a support staff position at a library, and the experience introduced me to librarianship as a profession. I hobbled together an understanding of the field through hours of reading email discussion lists, reading and contributing to blogs, and talking with colleagues. I jumped feet first into ALA to get an understanding of the profession and continued to work in a library full-time while I pursued my master's degree in library and information studies. Since graduating and becoming a librarian, I have gotten involved with every conference and library leadership opportunity I have time to participate in. This book distills my experience into something that is hopefully easier to digest, and in far less time, for people just beginning to think about librarianship and wondering whether this path might be a good fit.

My story is one of falling into the profession right out of college. Some of my colleagues knew from early ages they wanted to work in libraries, and others came to work in my library after full careers in other professions. The field as a whole is richer for this diversity of experience, and we are better able to meet diverse patron needs because of this.

This book is divided into four main areas of interest: the different types of libraries, the types of jobs, current issues in librarianship, and the things to keep in mind when getting started in the field. These four areas should help you understand librarianship and help you find the areas that you may prefer. Once familiar with the overview you will have enough information to have an idea about what you might like to pursue further. I have included resources lists for further information after each section of the book.

You are probably familiar with several types of libraries. In your childhood you likely visited school libraries or media centers. In college you almost certainly became familiar with your academic library. Along the way you have perhaps used a public library, too. These are three of the four major types of libraries. The fourth category of libraries is *special libraries*. These libraries exist in hospitals, law firms, businesses, and any other organization that needs someone to manage information, either coming from outside the organization or originating within it. The first section of the book will help you understand the different types of environments that are open to you in librarianship so that you can begin thinking of the type of library you might prefer as a workplace.

In addition to the different types of libraries they work in, librarians also hold a variety of positions. The second section of this book will help you understand what jobs are available and what librarians do in them. Though your first thought of librarians may be of people sitting behind a desk waiting to answer a question or check out a book, this image barely begins to represent the vast array of work within libraries. This section will show you the diversity of librarians' work.

If you have found the type of environment that you believe will be perfect for you and the job that looks interesting, you will undoubtedly face questions from your family and friends about the health of the field and your future prospects within it. The third section of this book will focus on trends in the field so that you will understand a few contemporary issues of librarianship. This section will provide some context to your understanding of the field by discussing the past and future of librarianship.

The final section of this book aims to help those who have decided that they would like to pursue librarianship. This section will address how to get started, giving you an explanation of how to find and apply for programs as well as tips to help you once you are in school. What you do outside of class while in library school helps prepare you for your first professional position as much as what you study during your program. Combining both your academic background with relevant professional experiences can make you more competitive for positions once you graduate from library school. This section will help you create a strategy for your time in school.

Libraries exist all over the world, and librarianship is an international field. Different cultures and locales have different expectations for their libraries and librarians. Because it would be nearly impossible to cover librarianship in the broadest sense, while being specific enough to help everyone, this book specifically addresses librarianship in North America. Explanations of libraries, positions, trends, and the graduate process describe the North American flavor of the field. Most libraries in North America require an ALA-accredited master's degree.

This field is an exciting one, where an interested and motivated person can really make an impact. Many of us find it to be a perfect fit. The field gives us an opportunity and reason to continue learning in our areas of interest. Librarianship allows us to help other people develop a love of learning and scholarship. The profession gives us a way to earn a living while making a positive impact on our community. It is not too good to be true. Over 100,000 of us do this work every day.[5] Keep reading to find out where you could work and where your career could take you.

---

[5] American Library Association. (2008). Number Employed in Libraries. Retrieved October 25, 2008, from http://www.ala.org/ala/aboutala/offices/library/libraryfactsheet/alalibraryfactsheet2.cfm.

Types of Libraries

Librarians work in a number of settings, and most tend to identify strongly with the environment in which they work. Librarians' work is broadly similar, but there are significant differences in our day-to-day work. This chapter will address the different types of libraries you could find yourself working in as a librarian so that you can begin to think about the type of library setting that may be right for you.

The skills of librarianship apply in any library setting, but some library work requires specializations that others do not. For example, expertise in children's literature would serve you well in school and public libraries, but not in most academic or special libraries. These specializations can make it challenging to move between different types of libraries throughout your career, though you can create opportunities to work in different environments if you desire to do so. If you think you might want to work in a different type of library later in your career, you can plan strategically and transferable skills when you look at other library jobs.

The four main types of libraries are school, academic, public, and special. All of these libraries collect, organize, preserve, and share information. Though they have much in common, there are differences as well. Librarians in these four types of libraries serve different communities and users. These users have varying expectations for the services and collections that the libraries offer. The nature of daily work for librarians varies as well.

School libraries, often called media centers, exist within primary and secondary schools. School libraries serve students from kindergarten through high school and meet students' literacy and research needs across this spectrum. School librarians buy books to support the curriculum, work with students, and teach classes. They work with school-teachers to make sure the collection meets the needs of the curriculum, as well as to teach students how to use the library for their assignments. One of the main goals of school libraries is to encourage literacy and a love of reading, so popular reading materials can be as important as the research materials available in the library. Finally, school librarians work with a young clientele. Because of this, they have to be particularly sensitive and aware of censorship issues and the appropriateness of the works they collect for their population and age groups.

Academic libraries share many traits with school libraries, but serve a more mature population with more complex research needs. Academic libraries serve a broad spectrum of institutions from community colleges to research universities. Academic librarians work with students on research projects in undergraduate to doctoral study in any number of disciplines. Academic libraries also serve faculty of the institution, aiding research in their fields of expertise. This means that academic libraries collect materials across a broad number of subjects, from introductory texts to scholarly communication intended for the research uses of the faculty.

Public libraries serve the public. These libraries provide materials and services to anyone in the community. Often, public libraries serve as places to get recreational reading, to do research and access the Internet, and to get research help from professional librarians. Work in these libraries differs and includes everything from story hour for toddlers to working with people one-on-one for genealogy research to teaching classes about research for small businesses. This work focuses on public service, and public librarians can see a direct impact of their work on their local community.

A special library is any library that does not fit in one of the above categories. These libraries exist in newspaper offices, law firms, hospitals, museums, and in a variety of businesses. Special libraries often exist to help the organization get its work done. Instead of teaching people how to do research, special librarians actually do the research, often writing up a report describing the findings. They might compile background information for a story in the newspaper or track down a list of diseases that present specific symptoms for a doctor. Special librarians may maintain the information of the organization, making sure people can get to institutional knowledge or research when they need it. These libraries exist as part of a larger organization and do not offer recreational materials. Special librarians sometimes have to prove that the library is useful to the larger organization.

Some of these libraries are more closely related to each other than to others. For example, school, academic, and public libraries all have education as a part of their aim. Academic and special libraries both have an interest in preserving institutional knowledge. School and public libraries both work on literacy issues and promoting a love of reading. All libraries are part of the larger culture that is becoming more focused on electronic resources, and might be adapting in light of these trends, though this is sometimes more obvious in academic and special libraries.

This chapter will focus in much greater detail on the different types of libraries available to you as a librarian. Of course, you do not have to know for certain where you would like to end up at this point. You have time to figure that out. In library school you can take entire classes about each type of library. You can also get practical experience through practicum or volunteer work. An understanding of the different types of library environments will help you understand where to work when you graduate, or at least help you identify strengths and weaknesses of each option for you and your personality.

Having an idea about what type of library is right for you will also help you to know where to look for jobs. Academic libraries advertise in very different places from special libraries, for example. While in school, you should monitor job advertisements to know what skills are sought by employers. Knowing which skills you might need to have will help you know what you should learn. At the end of this section, you will find a list of resources for finding more information about each type of library as well as where you can find relevant job advertisements.

School Media Centers

The school library is the first library that many people can remember visiting. You may recall a room full of bookshelves, "story times," a librarian who saved special books for your class' visits, or your first lessons in how to do research. These early library environments helped foster a love of reading or research. This formative experience undoubtedly warms many of future librarians to the idea of libraries, and later to the idea of librarianship. The role of a school librarian can be especially rewarding. These librarians truly can shape someone's reading habits for the rest of his or her life.

School libraries, often referred to as media centers, are the libraries associated with elementary, middle, and high schools. Within this specialization, there is a surprising amount of diversity in the work librarians do. School librarians work with students from kindergarten through the senior year of high school. School libraries are part of public or private institutions. Their users could be learning how to read or are applying to college.

School libraries tend to be very small with few staff members. Some school libraries have only one librarian, and depending on local laws, the librarian might not need an ALA-accredited master's degree. Larger school libraries sometimes have more than one librarian and both large and mid-sized school libraries might have staff without a library degree to work with the professional librarian. In any case, school libraries tend to be fairly small and run by a small staff. This means that when working in a school library you get to know every book in the collection. You can take part in every aspect of what the library does: selecting and ordering books, the technical work that goes into running the library, reference, and circulation. You are able to see every student in the school and you get to know every teacher and administrator. You can feel a sense of ownership over what the library does. You can have the satisfaction of running your own small organization.

School librarianship perhaps provides the last place in librarianship where you can truly know every book, volume, and issue in the library's collection. With just a few thousand items, you can remember the materials in the collection on most any topic, without referring to a catalog or other finding aid. When a user has a question, you can immediately know what you have that might help the user with their work. Depending on the layout of the library, you might be able to physically look at the shelves and see which areas are lacking and which are bursting at the seams. You are unlikely to gain this intimate understanding of a collection in larger public libraries, and you would not be able to do so in large academic institutions (other than perhaps in specific subject areas).

School librarians, working with smaller communities than other librarians often serve, are able to know their users very well. School librarians can get to know the specific information covered by their school's curriculum, and select materials that are particularly useful in these areas of study. In cases where the librarian teaches regular library sessions for all classes, the librarian can get to know every student in the school. This means they understand the reading levels, interests, and trends of their entire community and can get materials that are most appropriate for the student body. When a librarian has such a complete understanding of their students, they can make better collection management decisions for the collection. Many school librarians find this selection process to be one of the most rewarding aspects of their work.

Some school librarians have open periods, or times of the day when students can come in and use the library freely. Some school librarians teach special classes to students in order to help them with their research. Others have regularly scheduled sessions with classes so that students get continual library instruction in addition to their course work. School administration often makes the scheduling decisions about the school's library, with feedback from the school librarian and teachers.

School libraries can have unusual hours, as well. Some stay open just during the school year, during school hours. Others open a bit earlier than the start of school and stay open after school lets out throughout the school year. Still others stay open over the summer vacation in case students want to continue using the library before the start of the fall semester. Though you might know you want to be a school librarian, it would be difficult to know the schedule you are likely to work until you have selected a position and learned the school's policy on library hours.

Finally, you should remember that school librarians are teacher-librarians. They are often required to have a teaching degree in addition to the master's degree in library studies. This qualifies librarians to be classroom teachers in addition to school librarians. This credential can help the school librarian gain the respect of faculty. It also can give the librarian confidence when working with students in a classroom setting. If you are interested in school librarianship you should look into the local policies for the communities where you would like to work.

Users

The community that a school library serves is fairly small. The primary users of school libraries are students, but school librarians also work with the principal and school administration, teachers, and parents. As the library users tend to be minors, librarians have to think about their collection and balance freedom of speech and information with limiting their collection to the most appropriate materials for their community. School librarians should particularly pay attention to censorship issues. Understanding what books might be challenged, the reasons why certain books may cause controversy, and why the books could still be important for the collection can be very important if you are to ever face a book challenge.

Of course, students coming to the library for research or reading materials are the primary users of a school library. Sometimes school librarians work with specific students to find books at the right reading level and on an interesting topic in order to motivate students to read more. Other times, librarians will work with classes that come to the library to learn about the research process. These classes might have detailed assignments from their teacher that lead to the class coming to the library. School librarians work with students on their projects to teach them the steps in the research process and to build a strong foundation for the research they will do later in their academic career.

Librarians sometimes help build this foundation by teaching a session to a class working on an assigned research project. The librarian works with the class in order to demonstrate the research process and might pull relevant materials off the shelves for the students to use. Librarians also help build a strong research foundation by providing one-on-one help for an assignment, custom tailored to each specific student's needs and interests.

Librarians also play an important role in helping students learn how to read. The school librarian is not a student's primary teacher, which changes the nature of their relationships with the students. In some respects, librarians can become better friends with students than their primary teachers can, and for this reason librarians are able to reach students in a different way. Students can perceive the school librarians to be someone more like an aunt or uncle, whose main interest is helping students find materials that are really interesting. School librarians can help students realize their strengths and weaknesses and help draw out students by finding material that closely aligns with their personal interests. By providing interesting and popular titles, school librarians can help their users foster a love of reading from a very early age.

School librarians also work with the school's teachers. The better the relationship between the school librarian and the teachers, the better they can coordinate their efforts. As a librarian gets to know the subjects that teachers cover with their students, the librarian can improve the library collection in those areas. If the school librarian and teachers communicate well, the teachers can create curricula and assignments that make best use of the collection and the librarian's skill. School librarians may have a small collection of works for teachers on issues related to student development, education, and instruction techniques, providing further resources for teachers. The relationship between the school librarian and teachers is beneficial for the students, teachers, and librarian of the school. This relationship gives rise to better assignments, better learning, and, ultimately, better-educated students.

Student's parents are another audience for the school library. Parents who are invested in their children's education may have a special interest in the school library as a supplement to classroom learning. However, parents might also have strong opinions as to what their children should see and read in the school library. Some might ask the school to censor material or remove books from the collection. In these cases, the school librarian should be well versed in professional ethical values. On the one hand, the school librarian should serve the needs of the users, and there can be times when it is controversial materials that do that best. On the other hands, parents ultimately have responsibility for their children and rightfully want to have a say in what they can read or learn about in the library. If you should face a situation in this area, and there is a good chance that you will, you will have a number of resources available to help you, from professional associations and colleagues who have faced similar situations.

Some parents, looking to be involved in their child's education, may end up volunteering in the library. Some parents are interested enough in the library that they seek it out as their place to volunteer. In addition to these parent volunteers, some students like to be library helpers. Parent and student volunteers mean additional help to run the library, which can provide the librarian with an opportunity to focus on the more challenging aspects of library work. However, having volunteers does not mean the librarian has less work to do as these volunteers most likely perform different types of tasks. Some of a school librarian's work might typically be clerical in nature, including the processing of paperwork, shelving or pulling materials, or checking out books. When volunteers do this work, it frees up the librarian's time for more complex duties, but also requires a new set of management skills. School librarians might train volunteers to do these tasks and follow up to make sure they are done well. When working with parents, the volunteers might have significant accomplishments and experience in their own fields, so the librarian may choose to work with them to develop tasks that make use of considerably advanced skills. When working with students, the librarian might be creating students' first experiences as accountable employees. In this sense, school librarians help student volunteers to develop good work skills to be transferred to real jobs in their future.

Trends

The most significant challenge in school librarianship is funding. Some states are cutting budgets and some school districts are cutting positions. There are many reasons for budget challenges in school libraries, ranging from funding issues on the state level to a belief that the Internet makes it less important to have a comprehensive school library. However, research shows that school libraries and trained school librarians raise student achievement levels and the students' enjoyment of reading.[6] Research like this leads many states and districts to fund their school libraries even with the abundance of information online and through difficult budgetary periods.

The Internet impacts school librarians beyond creating a new need to make the case for funding. School librarians also have to adapt their teaching of research skills in light of new online tools and resources. Part of this adaptation is to help students learn the appropriate way to use the Internet for research. This can be challenging work in general, but particularly in schools that are required to have filters on their computers. Computer filters sometimes block websites that would be useful for research and will often block websites that students would find when doing research at home. This altered search environment makes it difficult to talk with students about how to evaluate all the resources they would find when doing research on a computer without a

---

[6] The Ontario Library Association. (2006). *School Libraries & Student Achievement in Ontario*. Retrieved October 25, 2008, from http://www.accessola.com/data/6/rec_docs/ 137_eqao_pfe_study_2006.pdf.

filter. The filters on school computers may also mean that a school librarian cannot use some of the online technologies that their librarian counterparts in other types of libraries are able to use.

Scheduling is another important part of a school librarian's position. There are two main types of scheduling in school libraries today: flexible and fixed. A school librarian might have a flexible schedule in which teachers can schedule a session with their class or in which students can drop by when they need to find something. This type of schedule can allow greater flexibility for working individually with students, but can also mean that students do not all get the same level of service. A school librarian has a fixed schedule if students come to the library, as a class, on a regular basis. In this environment, the librarian knows when students will visit, and can develop a year-long curriculum to train students and to add more difficult concepts over time. Teachers may or may not come with the class for library work. Many school librarians advocate that teachers accompany their class to reinforce the important points of the lesson with students later on and to prevent discipline problems from arising. School librarians do not always have the luxury of the teacher's presence in class, though, as these sessions are often scheduled to provide for the teacher's planning period.

A trend in school libraries has to do with what they teach. The core subject area for school librarians is "information literacy." This is the ability to find, evaluate, and use information. School librarians work with students to develop this skill both in the library and online. School librarians share this discipline with academic librarians. In both settings, librarians work with students to gain a basic level of competency in their ability to research and to build on the levels gained at earlier stages of their academic career.

Finally, school librarians have the very important role of a liaison. They liaise with the school administration, teachers, parents, and the community. School librarians have to work with school administrators to make sure the needs of the library are met. They work with teachers to collaborate on the education of students. School librarians market their services to parents to make sure that the community is aware of the materials and services they offer.

School librarianship can be an extremely rewarding specialization of library work. You have ownership of an entire collection and can work to shape it over time. School librarians have the opportunity to work with people just discovering the joys of reading. In this role, school librarians can be friendly and supportive adults for their students. Most of all, as a school librarian, you know that your work contributes to the future behaviors of your students. You know this because, in all likelihood, your school librarian played a role in getting you to where you are today.

Academic libraries

If you are thinking about becoming a librarian, and you are graduating from college, you are most likely very familiar with academic libraries. You have probably browsed in the sprawling stacks and used a number of the library-provided article databases. You may have gotten help from the librarian at the reference desk, or chatted with a librarian on the computer. You might even have had a student job shelving books, filing interlibrary loan requests, or working behind the scenes in the library.

Academic libraries appeal to people who enjoyed college. As an academic librarian you are able to work with faculty and college students. You can support significant, cutting-edge research while also helping students learn the steps necessary to do college-level research. You can also partici-pate in the research process yourself, writing articles and giving professional presentations. Some academic libraries expect this professional involvement in addition to regular professional duties.

There are many types of academic libraries. There are community colleges, small liberal arts schools, master's de-gree- granting colleges, and research universities. In any of these, your work will be impacted by the strengths of your institution. A large technology and science research institu-tion will have very different collections of materials, curric-ula, and research needs from a small liberal arts school. You should think about this if you would like to work with a spe-cific subject area. If you would like to further your own aca-demic study while working in a library, you might choose an institution with strengths similar to your interests.

In some institutions, academic librarians are considered faculty members on a tenure track; in others, librarians have faculty status without tenure; and in the rest, librarians are professional staff. There are benefits and drawbacks to each of these systems, and you should consider your professional expectations when applying for jobs. When a position is tenure track, you know that there is an expectation for you to be professionally involved outside the institution through publishing, presenting, and committee involvement. This can be rewarding and can give you a better idea of what faculty do, but can also take a lot of time. When librarians have faculty status they can often participate in campus committees and can get to know teaching faculty more closely—but this also takes time. When a librarian has professional staff rank, he or she may have more time for library work without the pressure of tenure, but may face a slightly greater obstacle to gaining the respect of some faculty members.

If you plan to work in an academic library, it will serve you well to learn about the structure of academic institutions and how decisions are made. In general, academic librarians report through the university's Provost, but they may interact with departments in other parts of the university. In such large organizations, for example, it is hard for a library to improve their online catalog or to begin digitization projects without the help of an Information Technology department, which may or may not be responsive to the library's needs. Librarians need to have the ability to communicate with faculty about purchasing decisions and to know what research needs exist within individual departments.

Though there are many similarities among academic libraries, each academic library is a little bit different, too. This section will address different types of academic libraries so that you can have a better understanding of the diversity within the field.

Community College

Community colleges grant two-year Associate's degrees and offer technical training such as automotive systems technology or coursework to prepare student to be an electrical engineering technician. These schools serve diverse populations. The student body can be comprised of advanced high school students, students wishing to reduce the overall cost of their college degree by attending community college for two years, students looking for specialized technical training, and returning students of many different educational backgrounds. These students come to the community college at a range of ages, with a variety of backgrounds, and with an assortment of expectations about what they might get from their education.

The faculty of community colleges do not have the research expectations that faculty have at college and research institutions. Faculty in these organizations emphasize teaching, and themselves come from a variety of educational backgrounds. Some have PhDs, some have master's degrees, and some have bachelor's degrees. Working with faculty at these organizations often is more centered on teaching and helping students learn to use the library than at other academic institutions.

The role of a community college librarian is similar to that of any academic librarian. If you choose this path, you will help students with their research, teach classes, and build a relevant collection. Your work will focus primarily on the student population since the faculty does not have strict research requirements, but that does not mean that your community is homogeneous. You will work with students from various backgrounds with a variety of goals.

Small Institutions

Many small colleges are liberal arts schools. These small colleges have correspondingly small libraries. Some may only have one full time librarian and others might have a small staff of librarians. These institutions allow for a closer relationship with students and faculty, and a diversity of experiences for library staff.

Small institutions tend to have fewer librarians, than larger institutions, so all staff get the opportunity to do more things. A librarian at a small liberal arts college may have a shift on the reference desk, teach classes in research and technology, repair damaged materials, negotiate deals with electronic vendors, and catalog incoming materials. This means that work is always interesting, and that there is always something new to do and learn, but it also means that librarians are not able to spend a majority of their time on any one duty.

It is worth noting that you can get amazing experience in these smaller libraries. By getting a breadth of experience you will gain a good understanding of the big picture issues in librarianship, and you would be able to take that with you should you pursue administrative positions later in your career. You can also get a good understanding of your strengths and weaknesses as well as areas in which you would like to develop. If you plan to go on to other positions later in your career, you will have broad experience to qualify for other jobs and you will know the areas of librarianship that you would like to pursue further.

Mid-sized Colleges and Universities

Between the very small colleges and the very large research universities, there are a number of institutions that that have a mid-sized student body and offer a few master's and doctoral degrees. These institutions have a lot in common with other small institutions, but they also have some of the research requirements of research institutions. The collections for these institutions must be a bit more robust in the disciplines for which they offer master's degrees, and the research questions that reference librarians might answer are often more complex.

As a general rule, universities tend to be comprised of a number of colleges and offer more advanced degrees than small colleges. Faculty at any institution are required to meet certain criteria in scholarship and research, teaching, and service. Some mid-sized institutions value teaching more heavily, while others balance teaching with more research. The collections in university libraries tend to be more comprehensive to support this level of research activity, and librarians tend to be responsible for fewer subject areas.

These institutions tend to be a bit larger than small liberal arts college libraries, with a larger staff. Though not the size of large research institutions, there are often enough full-time librarians that people are able to specialize in a specific type of library work, even if they occasionally have to fill in for colleagues in other areas. With more librarians comes a more hierarchical system, with mid-level managers. Though these libraries might have more hierarchy than a very small library, many of these institutions retain a relatively flat, team-based structure.

Mid-sized libraries offer their own benefits for library staff. Mid-sized staffs allow for quicker development of new services and collections. If the staff is large enough to offer specialization, individual librarians can often have ownership over the services they provide.

Research Universities

Research universities tend to have large libraries, expansive collections, and large staffs. In fact, many research universities have library systems that are comprised of a big central library and smaller, specialized branch libraries. While many smaller libraries have to worry about space restraints, paring down and weeding the collection, research libraries tend to keep materials. A book that might be weeded, or removed from the collection, in a smaller library because it is out of date might be relevant to a researcher in a research library who is tracing ideas over time or interested in cultural artifacts. Of course, keeping all this material means that large research libraries have to think about the issue of space as well, just in a different way than their smaller counterparts.

With the large staff often comes more hierarchy. Research libraries often have several levels of management, giving librarians the opportunity to move up within the organization. There are often a wide variety of departments, some of which might not be part of a smaller library, such as digital library development or marketing and outreach. Library staff members also tend to specialize in specific areas of work. This specialization can be very rewarding if you would like to develop in-depth expertise in a certain aspect of librarianship. It can also give you authority over a specific domain of work. Knowing that one area of the library's work is your responsibility allows you to claim ownership of that area. However, it also means that there are fewer opportunities to expand your work into other areas unless you pursue a lateral job transition.

In addition to supporting research needs, another main duty for research university libraries is to support the instructional needs of the students and faculty. Librarians work to strike a balance between serving the high-level research needs of faculty and graduate students while also meeting the needs of students. Some librarians work with

faculty to help design assignments, integrate library resources, and introduce research skills into their courses.

Working in research universities can also be quite rewarding if you like the idea of being involved in cutting-edge research. Some of the most well known scholars do their research from these institutions. You will directly support this
type of work if you work in an academic research library.

Users

The users of academic libraries tend to fall into five specific groups: students, faculty, staff, administration, and
community members. Everyone who works in a library
works to serve these users, whether writing collection development policies, helping find cataloging materials, creating
the systems that make research in the library possible, or
generating materials and answering questions.

The student populations of academic libraries vary
widely. Academic librarians help students at all levels of research skills, from eighteen-year-olds who have only used
Wikipedia for their research needs to doctoral students
working in obscure areas of research. Some of these users
have never used a library system before coming to the college library. Others have used several different academic
libraries and have expectations based on other experiences.

Faculty have needs specific to their work. Faculty members typically need to produce original scholarship as well as
teach their students. Libraries provide access to the existing
scholarship that faculty need in order to do their work as
well as access to the materials that they need to teach. Academic libraries are also beginning to explore open access
issues, and some are starting to offer services to faculty so

that they can have their own work archived, preserved, and even published by the library.

Academic staff and administration are also library users. Some staff members use library resources in order to find relevant information for their jobs. Information technology, counseling, and other departments rely on current research in their fields to develop best practices for the institution. Some non-academic departments, such as student affairs, might require publications and presentations of their staff members, so these staff members are also involved in their own research. Some academic staff pursue advanced degrees, and would use the library as students do.

Some academic libraries allow community members to use the library's collection and services. Publicly funded universities often are required to open their doors to the community, and government document collections are required by law to be open to the public.[7] Public needs vary widely. Some high school students use the library for research for their advanced classes. Others want open access to the Internet, or would like to read scholarly materials that the local public library does not provide. Though many academic libraries are open to the public, some private academic libraries do not allow outside visitors.

---

[7] US Government Printing Office FDLP. (2008). Legal Requirements. In *Federal Depository Library Handbook.* Retrieved from http://www.fdlp.gov/repository/individual-sections-of-the-handbook/chapter-2-legal-requirements/download.html .

Trends

Anyone interested in working in academic libraries should pay attention to trends in higher education. Any of these trends directly impact the work of the academic library. Academic librarians need to monitor the ways faculty choose to publish their research. As journals increase in cost, academic librarians look to for new publishing models and venues as possible solutions.

Another general trend in higher education is that students are diverse in their expectations of technology. Traditional students (recent high school graduates) grew up in a media-rich environment, using technology and the Internet for most of their lives. These students might never have seen a card catalog or a physical journal and lack that context for understanding how to use the library. At the same time, there is an increase in the number of non-traditional, returning students. The last time these students visited a library, the card catalog might have been the only way to find materials. These contrasting student bodies exist side-by-side in most institutions.

There is also a growing interest in online learning opportunities. Whereas primarily students studying at a distance once desired this type of education, students living on or near campus are now showing an interest in these options. Students who juggle multiple priorities often find online classes an option that affords flexibility, allowing them to work online when they have time.

These technological expectations also shift expectations of library services, leading to a preference for immediate online access to library resources, help, and answers. There is an increase in interest in digital content, from the *Google Books* project that helps digitally scan in many university collections to local libraries that digitize their own archives. As libraries increase their digital offerings, some redefine their roles on campus. Some libraries move parts of their collection off-campus to make room for more study space. Some experiment by offering more services and meeting the students where they are, in their academic departments and residence halls.

Like school libraries, academic libraries are interested in information literacy. Some teach information literacy any time a student comes to the reference desk. Some hold programming or information sessions for the community on information literacy issues for interested students. Some teach sessions as part of academic classes, and others teach credit-based information literacy classes. Most librarians try to teach information literacy through a combination of these methods.

Academic libraries can be extremely rewarding places to work. If you have an academic inclination, this can be the opportunity to stay in a scholarly environment for your entire career. You can see the impact you have when you help students, and that can be a great perk of the job. Academic libraries are also an excellent environment for people interested in gaining an additional master's or doctoral degree.

Public Libraries

Public libraries vary widely depending on the community that supports them. Some public libraries have strong community support and therefore are amazing community resources. These libraries offer information and services to all members of the community and are known as a gathering space for community members as well as for providing a place that holds relevant and valuable community resources. Other communities do not support their library to the same extent, and these libraries struggle with difficult budgets and have to make challenging decisions about how to provide a strong level of service and good collections.

Many public libraries exist as part of a system with a central location that has the ability to serve the most diverse clientele and branches to serve specific communities. The central library is the main branch, and often offers the strongest collection and a wide variety of programs and services. Branch libraries are located throughout the geographic area that the library system serves. The staff and collection can be quite small at branches, but the services and collections are, ideally, able to target the surrounding area's needs specifically.

Public libraries offer a wide variety of materials, from popular reading to resources for serious research. Public libraries support students with supplemental resources for school projects. They support community needs by providing information about local government and information useful to small businesses. Public libraries also provide entertainment, from popular reading to movies to, at some libraries, video games and gaming equipment. Most public libraries offer access to the Internet and computer programs that the community may need, such as Microsoft Word or Excel.

Public libraries offer other types of services as well. Most people know about basic public library services, such as answering reference questions or suggesting a good book to read for pleasure. But public librarians offer a number of other services, for entertainment as well as for strengthening the community. Some coordinate book clubs or offer programming for teenagers. Many offer a "story time" for young children and after-school homework help for stu-

dents. Some offer basic tax assistance for low-income patrons. Many public libraries try to use programming crea-
tively to bring atypical patrons through the door. They do
this in a number of ways, from hosting concerts to offering
gaming nights.

Organization

The organization of public libraries is built on the foundation of the local government. As most public libraries are
part of county or city systems, anything that impacts the
community impacts the public library. City councils, or the
county, determine budgeting, building needs, and can have
the ultimate say on upper-level hiring decisions. For this
reason, savvy public librarians pay attention to what happens in the local political scene, and library directors are
personally acquainted with local politicians and city council
members who influence the library's future. This political
knowledge can be very important for librarians.

In addition to the local government, public libraries often
work with Friends and trustee groups. These groups consist
of community members who have a vested interest in the
library and they work with the library to improve services to
the community. There are frustrations, as board members
likely do not have the library training and experience of
most library staff, nor do they face the requirement to earn
the master's degree in library studies. This difference in
background can lead to different viewpoints when making
decisions about the future of the library. However, board
members are great advocates, as they are devoted to the
library and its future. Friends groups sometimes also organize fundraising efforts to strengthen the finances of local
public libraries.

The size of public libraries varies greatly. Small communities tend to have smaller libraries. Larger communities tend to have larger ones. A system with many branches may have a lot of small libraries, while a system that chooses to focus resources on one central library might have one very large library.

The main branch of a large system typically has a large staff, with librarians specializing in specific types of work and subject areas. A small branch library, or a single library for a small community, sometimes has only one librarian in the entire building. Librarians in these settings have to be generalists in both the work they do and the subject matter the library supports. Depending on your disposition, you have a number of options within public libraries. You can specialize and "move up the ladder," and you can gain great administrative experience managing your own branch even early in your career.

Services

Public libraries are models of customer service. They understand that they have to illustrate their usefulness to the community to continue to exist. Many public libraries have explored user-friendly services for many years, and academic librarians are only now implementing some of these services. For example, some academic libraries are adopting the programming model that public libraries have used for some time. Public libraries can often innovate, particularly in branch offices that are located within specific communities. These small-scale libraries can serve as incubators and pilot locations for new and interesting ideas and services.

One way that the public library serves the community is through programming—workshops, presentations, displays, and activities. Public libraries offer programming as a way to bring the community together, to educate community members, and to help increase awareness of their services. These programs also allow librarians to reach out to the community and to provide a community space. In doing this they build stronger communities and make their mission clear to their users. They can create educational opportunities and help users find related material if they have an interest in a given subject. Through the creation of these educational opportunities, librarians are just as much educators as when they work at the reference desk or when they run a story hour.

A specialized type of program that is quite popular in public libraries is the book club. In these clubs, members of the community come together and read the same book in a given period of time, and then meet to discuss the book. Participants might choose popular books, books on a theme, fiction, or non-fiction. Sometimes reading programs are done on a larger scale. A public library might run a reading group along with Oprah's book club. They may create a city or county wide "same book" program, in which they encourage everyone in the community to read the same book. These clubs can encourage literacy on a large scale and can bring communities together around a theme. Not all book clubs are so structured, though. Some have the flexibility to focus on the interests of just the book club's participants. Some rotate the person responsible for selecting the book so that everyone has the chance to lead within the group.

In an effort to promote English language literacy, many public libraries focus on literacy initiatives for users who are not native speakers of English. Librarians sometimes create programming around learning English: they might create book groups for people with a more basic reading level, and they may bring in tutors to work one-on-one with users to improve their English skills. Public libraries also work to promote democracy through helping foreign-born users prepare for citizenship test, helping users learn about local issues, and providing information about voting.

Some foreign-born users have expectations of libraries based on their previous experiences. Some countries do not have freely available libraries; some libraries are not focused on the privacy of their users; and some only carry government-approved information. Public librarians serving users from other countries might have to educate their users as to how North American libraries operate and what they offer. Many libraries collect materials in secondary languages for their community so that they can provide services and materials to people who do not know English while helping them become familiar with the library. Libraries in some communities seek out multi-lingual librarians in order to have people on staff that can effectively communicate with all community members. Also, some communities offer language workshops in languages other than English. In these conversation groups, members can learn how to speak basic levels of secondary languages in their own communities.

In a similar vein, many public libraries realize the importance of computer literacy. Librarians in these communities offer classes in basic computer skills. This may seem out of the realm of typical library services, but by offering opportunities to gain basic proficiency in computer usage, librarians make patrons better equipped to use the Internet and to navigate today's information environment. These skills are increasingly important as more information goes online and as libraries begin buying online-only versions of some of their resources. Online resources are not useful to the patrons if they cannot use the computer to locate the materials. If the job of librarians is to facilitate access to information, then library staff has to make sure that the public is able to access the materials the library provides. Teaching patrons to use computers is not so different from teaching them to use the card catalogs of the past.

Many public libraries also look for ways to serve people who cannot or do not come to the library. One way libraries accomplish this is through the use of Bookmobiles. These traveling libraries can go to users at summer camps, schools, or local events, and provide users with access to materials and the chance to get to know their local librarian. Another way libraries reach users is by offering services to deliver materials to users who physically cannot come to the library.

Users

Public libraries serve the general public. This means they must keep a wide variety of people in mind. Public libraries serve the youngest members of the community to the oldest, the most financially secure to the least. They serve people in every career and vocation. They are also intended to serve all community members whether they walk through the library doors or not.

Parents often bring their children to the library for storybooks or reading materials. Libraries offer "story time" for young children, and children's librarians specialize in child development. The programming that children's librarians design is created to help young people develop and to advance their interest and love in reading from an early age. Some children's librarians offer programs for parents on child development and literacy. The programming that public libraries offer for young children tends to promote literacy from the youngest ages.

Young adult librarians work with the users older than children but younger than adults. They try to keep the library interesting to the group most likely to lose interest in it.[8] In an effort to retain these users, young adult librarians create advisory groups for teens to keep them interested and involved in the work of the library. They experiment in new areas of service, such as participating in social networking sites like MySpace and Facebook. They create themed events, such as Harry Potter parties. They organize game nights or video game tournaments. Young adult librarians who create these types of events and environments help young people think of the library as place that is "for them," with staff members to whom they can relate. If young adults learn this lesson well, they will remember the library in later years.

There are children, young adult, and adult student library users, too. In many cases, by the time a user gets into college, the academic library will better fit their needs. However, most public libraries are equipped to meet the research needs of students through high school. The public library supplements the school library, which might have limited hours and a smaller collection. In these cases a public librarian helps find answer to research questions for students, and also helps the student learn how to do research on his or her own.

Adult users come to the library for a number of reasons. Many adult users read for pleasure. They love reading and

[8] Snowball, C. (2008). Enticing teenagers into the library. *Library Review*, 57(1), 25 - 35.

use the library to get free access to books. They might want to find the most recent best seller, an audio book for their car, or a movie. Adults have different motivations for coming to the library than many of their younger counterparts. They already have developed a practice of reading, so they come to the library with an idea of what they need or would like to read. Many make use of reference services when starting their own business, working on genealogy research, or beginning a new home improvement project. The library can serve as a place to get useful information for beginning new projects or evaluating how a project is going.

Many public libraries want to be a "third place" for their users: the place patrons go when they are not at work or at home. Framing the library as an enjoyable place to be helps public libraries create service, modify facilities, and get materials that encourage library use.

Trends

There are also a number of trends in public libraries. Some communities are highly supportive of their libraries, building impressive new buildings and giving the library the budget necessary to provide a robust collection and a staff large enough to support the community's needs. Libraries, in these communities, are bustling centers of community activity, operating in great facilities, with plentiful staff and materials.

Other communities, faced with difficult financial situations, are cutting librarian positions and materials budgets. Some communities threaten to eliminate their libraries. Libraries in these communities face a number of challenges. In addition to limited collections, vacant librarian positions are sometimes reclassified as support staff jobs so that they do not require a master's degree and the higher level of pay that goes with it.

Many public libraries are on the cutting edge of serving patrons because they have to be. Offering excellent services helps the library make the case for the importance of its continued funding. Librarians in these institutions look for new ways to increase the public's awareness of the benefits of library services and collections, and do innovative work.

As a way of coping with severely limited resources, many public libraries partner with groups in the community. A library might work with small businesses, government agencies, public schools, or health centers to put on programming for the community or reach new users. Working with other organizations allows for community groups to pool resources to meet community needs.

Perhaps the most important thing about public librarians, though, is the role they play in the community. Public libraries provide a foundation for community education. If you choose to work in a public library you can truly impact the quality of life for your neighbors, friends, and family. In doing so you are able to combine making a living and making your community a better place to live.

Special Libraries

Special libraries exist to meet the needs of specific organizations. These libraries include every library except for the previous three categories—school, academic, and public libraries. Special libraries have much in common with other libraries, but there are a lot of differences as well. This section will discuss common aspects of special libraries and address some of the differences among them. Special librarianship appeals to many people. As a branch of librarianship, special libraries allow you to become an expert in the subject matter in which your library specializes, and to know you have a direct impact on the work of the organization.

Whereas most librarians aid patrons with their research needs and focus on helping their patrons learn how to do research themselves, special librarians often carry out the actual research and create reports for the organization. Special librarians support the mission of the business and help the organization get the information it needs in order to do its work.

Many types of special libraries exist. They are common in law firms, hospitals, and large corporations. They exist in prisons. State governments have special libraries and archives. Special librarianship is a broad area of the overall library field. This section will describe a few types of special libraries in order to give you an understanding of the differences and similarities among them.

Corporate

Most large companies have corporate libraries. Librarian positions within these organizations often have job titles that reflect the culture of the organization, such as "Information Specialist." Library staff members provide resources to help with research and development. Librarians in these roles have users, too, but their users are employees of the organization with specific research needs related to their jobs. To do this work, corporate libraries subscribe to appropriate journals and databases and keep current information on trends in their employer's field. Many of these positions deal with industry secrets and necessarily regard information as a competitive asset, so these librarians cannot participate in the traditional librarians' ethos of information sharing.

The people who special librarians work with are the employees of the organization. These users might work in research and development, where employees need to find the industry's latest research and information for new products. Special librarians might work with management to locate current best practices or employment laws and regulations that the organization must follow. As all librarians meet the needs of the user, special librarians work to meet the information needs of the corporation.

Special librarians tend to spend time writing reports. If you choose this environment, you will find the data for your colleagues, compile it in a report, and hand it off to the person who needs the information. This is quite different from the work done by school and college librarians, where the emphasis is in educating others in how to find information. Special librarians get the satisfaction of performing the research themselves. If you like thoroughly investigating an issue and synthesizing the findings, this environment might be an appealing one.

Medical

Medical libraries tend to be either clinical or academic. These libraries collect materials to support the practice of the institution's clinicians as well as the organization's research. To do so, medical libraries collect reference works, journals, and databases related to medical research. Medical librarianship can provide fulfilling work for people with a science background (though a science background is not always required) or those who would like to work in the health industry.

If you choose to work in medical librarianship, your users will be the institution's doctors, nurses, clinicians, researchers, and other non-clinical staff. In a clinical setting a user may just need to know the right answer, and fast. The work done by academic medical librarians is a bit of a hybrid between special librarianship and instructional librarianship. In these settings a librarian might work with students to teach them the best research strategies and help them learn about different resources.

Law

Law libraries exist within law schools, law firms, and government offices. These libraries keep legal code, law journals, and other documents detailing laws, regulations, and government policy. The collection might contain physical books and journals as well as subscriptions to electronic resources. Many law libraries require that their librarians also hold a Juris Doctor's degree in order to ensure that they fully understand the role of the law and legal practice.

As with any library, law librarians serve their community. In law schools, law library users are the professors and students of the institution. In a law firm, law librarians serve attorneys and paralegals. In both cases law librarians find legal information based on user needs, whether the user needs information due to a case or an assignment. In academic institutions, law librarians help students learn to do research, while in law firms the librarian may write documents on the issues covered in a specific case.

Law librarians at law schools may teach required research classes for all law students. Positions in law school libraries are hybrid positions with characteristics of both academic and special libraries. You might do as much instruction as legal research in a law library, which may allow you to bring together two different areas of interests.

Newspaper

Some special libraries operate within newspaper offices. The librarians in newspaper libraries perform a number of functions. They keep files of local information so that reporters can gather needed facts when writing stories. They subscribe to national news wires for up-to-the-minute information on national news. They archive their own material for future use through microfilm and digitization. They the newspaper's own articles in a detailed fashion so that they can find everything that a paper has published on a topic over a given period of time, which can be useful in writing future news stories.

Newspaper librarians interact with newspaper staff as well as community members. They sometimes carry a pager in case an important story breaks and reporters need more background information. They find all the relevant materials for reporters on a given topic so the reporter can focus on gathering new information and on writing. Newspaper librarians sometimes work with community members who might be looking for an older story on a topic or for a specific photograph that they remember seeing. Sometimes the newspaper staff grants copyright permissions for the use of copyrighted materials in other contexts.

Newspaper librarians get to know a lot about local news stories and can provide instant access to information on given topics of interest. They perform a service for other institutions by preserving the work of the newspaper. For those who like cutting edge news and enjoy doing in-depth research, this field can be a perfect fit.

Other special libraries

There are many different types of special libraries. In highlighting a few, I hope you will gain a better idea of some of the things you might expect in a special library environment. Truthfully, there are so many types of special libraries that I cannot cover them all. There are libraries in prisons, where the work is more about literacy and education and can involve the stresses that you might expect in that environment. There are toy libraries that collect, preserve, and index toys much as a museum would. There are association libraries. The American Library Association has a library than collects, preserves, and indexes the work of the organization over time. Because of the characteristics of special libraries, and because they tend to be small institutions, special librarians have found a need for a professional association other than the ALA. They have created an organization called the Special Library Association. This organization works to provide professional development and support to special library workers.

The Work of Special Librarians

One of the biggest differences between working in a special library and working in other types of libraries is that in a special library the organization sees the librarian more as an employee of the corporation than a librarian. An organization with just a few librarians may have such a small population that others do not understand the librarian's role.

The aim of special librarians diverges from other librarians as well. Instead of educating, special librarians find information. Instead of promoting open access to information, special librarians sometimes need to guard the organization's information from competing interests. Much of the work special librarians do is based around writing reports and creating polished papers, rather than working one-on-one with a user on a research project. However, there are also special libraries in academic institutions that focus on educating the user for future research needs.

Though different from traditional library work, special librarianship can be exciting. Work that in some cases warrants the use of pagers illustrates that special librarians work on the cutting edge of what is happening in their fields, and gives a level of importance to their work. Special librarians may also have additional qualifications such as a JD or a medical degree. The work in these environments can be highly stimulating and intellectually challenging.

The special librarian is often the only librarian in his or her library, or is part of a small staff. In this role, special librarians do not have as many colleagues to turn to for assistance or support on as they would in an academic or public library. In many cases an individual runs the library on his or her own. This level of independence is empowering, but can cause stress. At those times, it is worth knowing that organizations exist to support you if you choose one of these positions. These organizations can give a solo special librarian a network of people to provide feedback and suggestions from colleagues in similar situations.

Special librarianship is the most diverse area of librarianship. It gives you insight into how the world at large behaves and what it expects. It lets you operate in fast-paced environments. It can be cutting edge. It can also provide challenges that let you prove your worth every day of the job.

Special librarianship also gives you multiple identities. Rather than just identifying as a librarian, you are a librarian within an organization. You may have a better salary, and you will probably work under more stressful conditions. But if you like fast-paced, output-oriented work, special libraries might just be the place for you. The work special librarians do makes a difference in their organizations.

Trends

Though these libraries are very different, you can still find trends associated with them. This section will address some of the issues common to Special Libraries.

As with all libraries, special librarians try to understand how the shift from physical to digital materials impacts them, their work, and their professional lives. Some special libraries buy more electronic materials. Some digitize their own content. Changes in their collections can lead to changes in the physical library and staffing patterns, as well.

With more and more information going online, many special librarians have to make the case for their existence. It is important to understand the value that special libraries add to the overall organization. As budgets are cut and materials increase in price, the organization's financial officers may see the library as a prime candidate for elimination in harsh times. For that reason it is very important to illustrate what the library brings to the organization. Fortunately, the library may be able to save the organization money by pooling resources in one location, and the library can save time through streamlining research and providing accurate information for research and development.

Another trend is the implementation of knowledge management systems. These systems allow people to save institutional knowledge locally, so that if an employee is absent or another employee needs to make contact with a client, the information is stored within the organization. Organizations experiment with a variety of knowledge management software, from out-of-the-box systems that institutions purchase to open source wikis. Special librarians working with these systems educate users so that they can contribute to the knowledge-base and use it to find information when they need it. These systems can help people do their jobs better as well as help in running useful reports.

Overview

At this point you should have a basic understanding of school, public, academic, and special libraries. Within each type of library there is surprising diversity. Some are large and some are very small. The users of a library vary depending on the community and purpose of the library. The funding available depends on the school, government, or organization that supports the library. When thinking about the type of library you might ultimately like to work in, realize that they are all a little different. Take time to see different libraries and talk with librarians about their work.

Also, realize that you are never trapped within one library setting. The master's degree in library studies prepares you for any library work, so if you start in one type and do not like it, you can always find a position in another type of library. It can sometimes be a little difficult to make these transitions, however. For example, a school librarian with an extensive understanding of children's literature might not be the most competitive candidate for an academic library position. However, if that librarian wanted to move to the academic setting, a good strategy would be to focus on information literacy, education, and pedagogy, as these skills are highly valued in many academic libraries.

Finally, if you want further reading to help you decide on the type of library you will want to work in, please see the references at the end of this chapter. You will find references to other sources of information about different types of libraries. Most library schools also offer courses in the four main categories of libraries.

Organizations

The American Library Association (ALA)
http://www.ala.org/
ALA is the main organizations for librarians in North America. ALA accredits the master's programs that prepare librarians for the field, advocates for libraries on the national and international level, and hosts two annual conferences. ALA is an umbrella organization that includes a number of other organizations including AASL, ACRL, and PLA.

The American Association of School Librarians (AASL)
http://www.ala.org/ala/mgrps/divs/aasl/index.cfm
AASL is the primary organization for school librarians. They hold conferences, publish and produce journals, and provide resources to support the work of school librarians.

Association of College and Research Libraries (ACRL)
http://www.ala.org/ala/mgrps/divs/acrl/index.cfm
ACRL is the main organization for college and research libraries. ACRL produces standards for library work, hosts conferences, and produces publications.

Public Library Association (PLA)
http://www.ala.org/ala/mgrps/divs/pla/index.cfm
PLA exists to support the work of public libraries. They also
host conferences and produce publications for their members.

Special Libraries Association (SLA)
http://www.sla.org/
SLA is the one organization in this list that is not part of
ALA. SLA is a stand-alone organization that was established
to meet the needs of special librarians. SLA also hosts conferences and produces publications for their users.

Medical Library Association (MLA)
http://mlanet.org/career/index.html

American Association of Law Libraries (AALL)
http://www.aallnet.org/

Further Reading

All Libraries

American Libraries
http://www.ala.org/al

Library Journal
http://libraryjournal.com

School Libraries

Knowledge Quest:
http://www.ala.org/ala/mgrps/divs/aasl/aaslpubsandjo
urnals/knowledgequest/knowledgequest.cfm

School Library Media Research:
http://www.ala.org/ala/mgrps/divs/aasl/aaslpubsandjo
urnals/slmrb/schoollibrary.cfm

Academic Libraries

College and Research Libraries:
http://www.ala.org/ala/mgrps/divs/acrl/publications/c
rljournal/collegeresearch.cfm

College & Research Libraries News:
http://www.ala.org/ala/mgrps/divs/acrl/publications/c
rlnews/collegeresearch.cfm

Public Libraries

Public Libraries Magazine:
http://www.ala.org/ala/mgrps/divs/pla/plapublications
/publiclibraries/index.cfm

Special Libraries

Information Outlook:
http://www.sla.org/io/

Types of Jobs

Many different types of professional positions exist within libraries. There are jobs that interact with the public and jobs tucked away in back rooms. Some jobs require teaching classrooms full of people, and other jobs require coding on the computer. Librarianship, as a field, offers a number of types of work. If you like the idea of working in a library, you will be able to find a job that fits your personality.

This chapter seeks to explain the variety of jobs available once you have earned a master's degree in library studies. The positions are grouped into general categories. In most large libraries these categories align with the organizational departments, though smaller libraries might choose to combine responsibilities in different ways. Understanding the work of a department and the different positions within librarianship will help you figure out the best fit for your personality.

To understand the different jobs that librarians hold it is useful to understand the hierarchy of a typical larger library staff. These libraries are typically organized around the type of work that each group performs. Within these units, positions exist at varying ranks.

Most library employees do not hold a master's degree in library studies and are typically not called "librarians." There are student employees and volunteers who often do a lot of the routine work such as checking in and out books and shelving materials. "Para-professional" or "support staff" work is typically done by full time employees who do not possess a master's degree in library studies. Though support staff members are not librarians, without them the library could not function. These positions range from clerical to student supervision to staff training positions. Libraries often include professional positions that do not require a master's degree in library studies, such as accountants, web designers, and marketing specialists. These employees may hold advanced degrees, though not necessarily in library studies.

Within the librarian staff, there is hierarchy as well. Many professional librarians work in a specific area. These positions might include reference librarians or catalogers. These staff members focus their work in their area of expertise within librarianship. Librarian's positions typically pay more than non-librarian's positions, and may involve supervision of students, volunteers, or support staff. Depending on the size and structure of the library, there may be a middle management layer consisting of team leader positions, heads of departments, or assistant directors. Many of these jobs still include some of the work that is done in front-line positions: hours on the reference desk, teaching library instruction sessions, or collection development responsibilities. However, these positions require the librarian to supervise the work of a group or department, in addition.

Library administration is ultimately responsible for a library or an entire library system. In smaller libraries, the administration might consist of a single library director. In larger ones there may be an administrative team. This team might include several people who directly report to the director. This team manages the business side of the library, from fundraising to facilities issues to budgeting and hiring for new positions.

It is common for librarians with management duties to continue participating in some specialist work throughout their career. Some managers like to work an hour or so at the reference desk in order to keep in touch with the work of their users. Others may continue ordering materials, or cataloging a small part of the collection, to stay informed on library processes. Some administrators in academic settings will teach classes. This practice helps keep library managers and administration familiar with users and their needs.

Libraries are governed in various ways. Some libraries operate much as a business would, with managers making decisions that others must follow. Other libraries, particularly academic libraries in which librarians have faculty status, operate with more of a shared governance model. In these institutions all librarians have some role in the management of the library. All librarians share in the decision making for the organization, in contrast to librarians working in a business-minded model.

With this basic understanding of library staffing, one should note that the Master of Library Studies is really a type of management degree. There are plenty of positions within libraries that do not require the master's degree if you just want to work in a library. If you want to work in a library and have the opportunity to give input in the direction the library should go, if you want a promotion path, or if you want to supervise people, the master's degree will be an important qualification. Entry-level librarian positions are mid-level within the organization, and inherently have more responsibility tied to them than the non-master's degree jobs do. If you can see yourself spending several years, or your entire career, in libraries, the master's degree in library studies would serve you well.

Understanding both the different types of libraries and the different types of positions in libraries can help you understand which area of librarianship is right for you. The next sections will discuss the different types of positions you can find in libraries. You should note that, in general, the larger the library, the more likely positions focus in just one area. Smaller libraries have fewer employees; librarians working in them often share duties across specializations.

Public Service

When most people think of librarians, they think of the people with whom they interact when they enter a library. Public service staff members check books out to users and answer their questions at the reference desk. They teach classes, plan and host programming, and work in departments dealing directly with patrons and their needs. These staff members interact with the public.

Not all public service staff members are librarians. Some are support staff: library employees who do not possess a Master of Library Studies but who still do library work. Circulation staff (also called access services staff), who check books in and out and maintain the stacks, largely fall into this category. Most of the people you would see at the reference desk are reference librarians with a master's degree. In fact, reference librarians in academic libraries sometimes have a second master's degree in an academic subject. Ultimately, public services staff members interact with the public, but may or may not be librarians. This section will discuss the different duties that public service librarians do and the work that takes place in public service departments.

Reference

Reference librarians are specialists in finding information. Most users know them as the librarians who sit at the reference desk and help patrons find answers. This is just one part of a reference librarian's job. Many reference librarians offer one-on-one research help, teach classes, and may specialize in a given subject.

While still performing traditional reference duties, reference librarians look for ways to adapt their services to today's electronic information environment. The approaches vary based on the communities served, but there has much innovation in this area in the past two decades. Some reference librarians have expanded their physical domain out beyond the reference desk, roaming through the library to answer questions the way attendants help customers in retail stores. Others have offered reference outside of the library building, in various places in the community or on campus where people need help finding information. And some librarians have even begun offering reference services on the Internet, providing research help via instant messaging, *Skype*, and even in *Second Life*.

Though the specifics of reference services vary according to community needs and interests, there are some common themes. The goal of the reference librarian is to help the user to find and access useful information. Sometimes reference librarians help in simple ways, by pointing someone in the direction of the restroom or logging them on a computer. Other times people need help navigating the library or its website to find materials that they know the library owns. However, many reference librarians most enjoy helping users with their research.

Patrons working on research issues come to the reference desk knowing that they need information about starting a business, writing a paper, or tracking down information about their family tree. In these instances librarians conduct a "reference interview." In a reference interview, the librarian asks questions to tease out what a patron specifically needs. A patron might come to the desk and say something like, "I need to find some articles on sports in China," but really needs information about basketball in Asia, with at least three scholarly articles for a five-page paper. Once the librarian fully understands the patron's needs, the he or she can help the patron define an appropriate topic for a five page paper, find resources that will provide all the information they need, including at least three scholarly articles, and help the patron evaluate the information sources that they come across together in a search. The result of this process can quite different from what the original question would suggest!

If you are interested in reference librarianship, you will want to learn about how to do good research. Learning about basic reference books, databases, and tips for advanced searching using the library catalog and the Internet will help you in this process. Many reference librarians teach classes in research skills, too. Some experience teaching will help prepare you for these positions.

Instruction

Instruction is a growing area of librarianship. School media specialists and academic librarians have traditionally provided library instruction. Increasingly, and particularly in academia, library instruction is developing as an important part of librarians' duties. This is in part because as information sources proliferate, finding and identifying the best, most relevant resource becomes more important. Information is easier to find—sometimes too easy to find. Since it is everywhere, and anyone can publish to the Internet, information availability grows quickly and without quality controls. Librarians specialize in finding high quality information, and, accordingly, often teach classes in how to be a good researcher. Librarians also teach classes on uses of technology, ranging from basic computer literacy to more advanced techniques in information retrieval.

In academic libraries, classes vary from single sessions for a particular instructor to semester-long courses. Professors typically request library instruction sessions for their classes, also called "bibliographic instruction" or "library instruction" sessions, to assist students with a specific paper or assignment. Librarians use these sessions to teach students about resources that could prove useful for the assignment, such as how to use subject-specific databases and how to approach the research process.

Sometimes librarians teach semester-long courses in information and research literacy for academic credit. These classes teach students general research skills that are applicable across many disciplines and contexts in order to be useful from the student's first year to years after graduation. A few institutions also teach subject-specific information literacy or information theory courses.

School librarians teach, as well. In fact, many are required to have an education degree in order to work as a school librarian or media specialist. School media centers can be programmed on a fixed or flexible schedule. Flex schedule school librarians teach classes when teachers request them. Fixed-schedule schools have regular schedules in which classes are scheduled to visit the library regularly. In fact, fixed-schedule librarians see all students in the school. Fixed-term schedules allow librarians to continually build on the lessons that students have had, creating an information literacy curriculum through the students' education in the institution. Flex-schedule librarians teach research at the point of need, when the teacher schedules it.

Public libraries often teach skills classes focused on how to use specific software, hardware, or research skills such as genealogical research. These classes are offered as programs for the public and vary based on interest and local needs. Some libraries even offer community interest classes in crafts or hobbies in order to bring more community members through the door and to showcase the library's collection on the topic.

Young Adults/Children

Though young adult and children's librarians are not formally given instruction librarian titles, they do have responsibility for specialized instruction. Through one-on-one relationships with their younger patrons, they help shape reading behavior from an early age and set students on a path to do good research through their adult lives. Young adult and children's programming can be designed around study groups; their librarians can work with them on skills specific to their age and experience.

Young adults and children's librarians provide programming to the community and work directly with parents and their children, as well. Children's librarians often focus on child development, creating programming targeted at specific developmental stages in order to help with children's growth. This programming may focus on physical development, literacy, or social development. One example of this is "story time," with age-appropriate stories, vocabulary, and call-and-response with the young audience.

Young adults and children's librarians might partner with school librarians, too. When students need to use the library after the school has closed, they go to the public library. Their librarians might teach them to use resources, databases, and basic research principles, just as their school librarian would during the school day.

Young adult or teen librarians often work with teen groups and advisory boards in order to create an atmosphere in which teens feel some ownership and involvement in their part of the library. These librarians actively create opportunities in which teens feel welcomed and interested. Teen librarians host gaming events, participate in online social networking sites, and are pushing libraries to embrace a wider variety of formats. Many teen librarians advocate for inclusion of graphic novels within their libraries' collections. This is important work, as today's teen users become the adult users—and taxpayers—of tomorrow.

Access Services

Access services combines several areas of library work. Access services staff members make sure the collection is in the right place and shelved, provide reserve materials for classes or groups, and interact with any patron that checks something out from the library. These staff members manage the collection.

Interlibrary loan is often located within access services departments. This department will find materials for patrons in other libraries. If the local library does not have something a patron needs, interlibrary loan will find the nearest copy and borrow it on behalf of the user. It is an amazing service that changes the library from being confined to one room or building to being a world of books and materials.

Reserves are an important part of an academic library. This department provides students with the readings that their professors have assigned them. Library staff members operating in this area work with faculty to reserve their materials, and generally make sure students have what they need. Course reserves are increasingly offered online, which means that staff members working in reserves also have to understand a little bit about copyright, digitization, and technology.

Finally, the access services unit that is most familiar to library users: circulation. This is the last place users go in the library before leaving with a book. Circulation staff check materials out, ensure library policies are followed, and deal with money if a patron has fines or needs to purchase something. Circulation staff members often do not have the master's degree, but are supervised by a librarian. Librarians in these departments may supervise a number of people, resolve issues as they arise if the front line staff are not able to, and work with administration on library policy.

When most people think of the library, they think of access services staff. If you are interested in being the face of the library, this can be a rewarding area of work. You would need to know about customer service, copyright issues for interlibrary loan and reserve work, and management, as in larger departments you would likely supervise other library staff members.

Overarching Similarities

All public services librarians work with library patrons and aim to create positive user experiences. Many work directly with student or volunteer workers, too. This means that public services staff members hire, train, supervise, and evaluate student workers and volunteers. This experience is useful for librarians interested in moving into management positions, and also provides the librarian with a useful view of the student body and community.

Public services staff members, whether librarians, support staff, or student workers, are the face of the library for the users. They create the user experience with their attitude, skill, and presence. They interact with users in a way that is much more intense than library administration or any of the behind-the-scenes library staff. If you enjoy interacting with people, public services can be a fulfilling area of librarianship. You can get to know people from all different ages and walks of life, and get to see a measurable impact that you can have on another's life. If you feel your calling is working with real, live people, and you enjoy directly helping them out, public services could be exactly the type of work that you would enjoy.

Technical Services & Collection Management

Technical services happens behind the scenes. The technical services department tends to be a large part of the library staff, but the average user may not even know that they are there. Technical services staff members are the heart of a library. They purchase materials, add records to the catalog, create collection management policies, and negotiate for electronic database contracts. They support everything else that happens in the library, and for that reason, even if they do not regularly interact with users, they are extremely important to the library's day-to-day operations.

This section will describe the different duties that fall under the category of technical services. Technical services departments can be very small or very large, depending on the organization. These departments tend to have a large number of support staff in addition to librarians. In fact, in many libraries this department may have the largest number of support staff members.

Technical services is exciting not only because it builds the foundation for all other library work, but also because this part of the profession has been fairly forward-thinking. Well before most people had thought of using computers to communicate and share information, technical services librarians were using them to share MARC records (the basis of the online catalog). Today, websites like *Library Thing* and *GoodReads* have users who catalog their own books for fun. If this type of work is interesting to you, you might find a place in technical services.

Collection Development

Collection development librarians work to build and maintain the collection. They develop the policies for purchasing or licensing materials, they create plans for removing dated or irrelevant materials from the collection, and they work with students and faculty to select materials for purchase.

Some librarians find collection development to be the most rewarding area of their work. Collection development allows people to get to know the current research in a field, as one would in graduate school, without having to specialize to the level that would be necessary to write a thesis or dissertation.

Collection development can be a challenging but intellectually interesting area of library work. In order to know what materials to include in the collection, librarians have to cultivate an understanding of the discipline and its publishing trends. Those who chose their major because the subject was interesting, rather than because of the job prospects that would follow, sometimes have the opportunity to collect materials in their areas of interest.

In addition to collecting physical materials, librarians are looking into ways to develop collections using materials in a variety of formats. This part of the field is changing rapidly, and many vendors are creating new and interesting ways to provide access to digital content.

As most libraries are bursting at the seams and it is difficult to find additional storage space, weeding, or removing books, becomes an increasingly important aspect of library work. Librarians have to determine which parts of the collection should be eliminated either because of the publication of newer information, because the collection does not best fit the needs of the current users, or because user needs adapt with changes in the curriculum or local community interests. Collection development librarians not only purchase new materials in their subject area, but also remove materials that became less relevant to user needs.

Acquisitions

Acquisitions staff actually purchase library materials. The collection development librarians, or the library staff members who are responsible for collecting in a specific area, place orders for materials, and acquisitions staff perform searches for the best prices and editions, and purchase the materials. Acquisitions may work with library vendors, mainstream book and movie vendors like *Amazon*, specialized or independent publishers, or rare book dealers in order to attain the needed materials for the collection.

In addition to individually selected titles, many libraries have approval plans. These plans automatically select certain materials, based on call number range or publisher. Since the library preorders titles from library vendors, librarians often get a better price on approval plan materials. Librarians also save the time they would have spent selecting and ordering the materials if there were not using an approval plan. Imagine a public library that always purchases the *New York Times* bestsellers. Including these books on the approval plan means they will always come to the library without someone dedicating time to order them.

Serials

Serials librarianship is complex enough that most mid- to large-sized libraries have at least one dedicated serials librarian. Serials are publications with recurring issues that are published with no predetermined ending. Magazines, newspapers, scholarly journals, and recurring reference titles are all serials. Serials do not always come out as reliably as they are scheduled to, and they continually come through the library door or the library's website. Over time the same publication may change titles, causing challenges for maintaining the catalog.

Serials librarians work with periodicals to make sure the catalog reflects them accurately so that when users look for all the holdings of a particular title they will find them, regardless of whether the publication has changed its title at some point in the past. Serials staff members also follow up on issues of a periodical that the library should have received but did not, registering a "claim" with the publisher or distributor.

Cataloging

We could not locate materials on the shelves if it were not for the library catalog. Catalogers create computer records for every item purchased by the library. Sometimes librarians download these records from OCLC[9] and modify them in a few ways before adding them to the catalog, a process known as copy cataloging. Cataloger librarians also create these records based on the materials themselves when unable to locate suitable records in OCLC.

When a library collects rare or unique materials, pre-existing catalog records usually do not exist. In these cases librarians must create original catalog records, usually using the MARC format; these are known as "MARC records." MARC records describe materials in a number of ways, from title to author to physical description to subject content. Library staff members add these records to the database that runs the catalog; then, users can find the items based on the information contained in the records.

When libraries purchase more generic materials, they can often purchase the MARC records for them from OCLC. This way of adding records is called "copy cataloging," since the main part of the work is copying records created by others. Support staff sometimes do this work, and in these cases librarians with masters degrees supervise this process. This work sometimes happens outside of technical services. For example, many libraries have separate government documents collections that operate as independent

---

[9] OCLC is the Online Computer Library Center, an organization that enables libraries to share cataloging records so that librarians do not have to create a record for an item that another library has cataloged.

libraries within the larger library. Most government documents can be copy cataloged and are processed by support
staff within those departments

Electronic Resources

Technical services departments often include electronic
resources librarians. (Sometimes electronic resources librarians are part of the reference department.) These librarians
work with the online books, journals, and databases. These
resources are a rapidly growing part of many libraries' collections.

If you are interested in becoming an electronic resources
librarian, you will work with the vendors, contracts, and
technical issues that arise with electronic resources. You
would work with the resource providers to make sure that
you are able to secure the resources and that they are accessible to your user population. As many libraries transition
large parts of their collections to electronic books, journals,
and databases, many libraries clearly value these skills.

Electronic resources librarianship begins to merge with
technology work, too. As surveys find that many users prefer
simpler search options for materials across different databases, electronic resources librarians also work closely with
technologies and library technology staff to provide easier
access options to their users.

Other Technical Services

Technical services is the department that orders, receives,
and catalogs materials. In addition to the above duties,
technical services has several other responsibilities. For example, library staff members have to add call numbers to

materials and identify materials as property of the library. This work often falls to support staff or students in the technical services department. When several issues of a periodical title are on the shelf, libraries often bind the issues into hardback books and move them to the stacks. The technical services staff prepares materials for this process. When people donate books to the library, they go through technical services and the subject specialist to see if the materials are a good fit for the collection.

Some technical services duties are distributed to other areas of the library. The government documents staff may do some copy cataloging, or the public services staff might prepare materials for the bindery. Subject specialists, in all departments of the library, tend to share collection development decisions. Technical services, as it builds the foundation for all library work, has to be done in a number of places throughout the library, so in all likelihood, even if you are not working directly in technical services, you will do some of this type of work. In fact, a strong understanding of how the library is organized, how call numbers work, and the organization of the records in the catalog provides a strong background for any library work.

Recently, the field has seen increasing discussion of automation within libraries. These conversations often focus on the work of technical services. Copy cataloging and approval plans have historically saved librarians time that would have otherwise been spent cataloging or selecting materials, and people have seen other ways that this type of automation and outsourcing could go further. Some libraries purchase materials that are already labeled and marked as property of the library. Some have outsourced collection development choices. Libraries are moving towards more streamlined ordering, removing excess steps from the process and placing requests using the same software that the acquisitions department uses to order materials. Some of these trends have been controversial, and more controversial suggestions are being made, such as the idea of outsourcing cataloging in general or relying on user generated information such as we see in online sites like *Amazon*, *LibraryThing*, and *Google Book Search*. Of course, discussions about automation and outsourcing are often contentious, and cause us to think about which duties require a librarian's expertise, knowledge of the community, and attention to detail.

The field does seem to generally agree that local librarians understand their communities best, and can create the most appropriate collection management policies, finest catalog records, and an unsurpassed framework for the local community's research and reading needs. Everything the technical services department does builds on this foundation, and it is an integral part of the library's service.

Rare Books and Archives

Many patrons find the rare books and archives collections to be the most enchanting areas of the library. How many times in your life can you touch something that is over three hundred years old? Or see the actual handwritten correspondence of a favorite author? Or hold a pom-pom that belonged to the first cheerleaders at a school? This tangible aspect captivates users and draws many people to archives and rare books librarianship.

Very few places in the library are still focused on the book or manuscript where information is contained in print format. Most places in the library focus on the information itself. A reference librarian will find an article just as useful if it is in electronic form or in a paper journal. However, rare books and archives librarians focus just as much on the physical artifact itself as the information therein. For this reason, people who love the actual object of the book often find themselves interested in and focused on archives and rare books.

Rare Books

Rare books include books that are rare for a variety of reasons. A rare books collection may include a book from the fifteenth century, a very small book made entirely of metal, a first edition of a classic work, and original papers from scholars, writers, or political figures. The common factor is that the materials are highly unusual and valuable. Libraries that collect rare books tend to collect in specific subject areas, which means the librarians in charge of these collections are experts in these subject areas. A library might focus on regional literature and history, a genre, or a specific writer. Librarians often base these decisions on the research strengths of the university or research institution.

Rare books librarianship requires knowledge of the publishing industry and book history, as well as an understanding of the value of different materials. Rare books librarians need to know when the library should spend a large sum of money on a book or when it should purchase something in its first print run. These skills may take a while to develop through both research and apprenticeship.

The library has to have a reason to collect rare books in a specific area, and therefore you will see trends in what a specific library collects. Once a library has developed a specialty in a given area, scholars located in other places may know them and travel to do their research. Some patrons of rare books and archives collections visit from across the United States and the world in order to work on research in a specific area. In these cases you might provide specialized research and reference assistance to these users.

Archives

Archives are collections of records about an institution. Many universities, communities, and businesses collect materials about their past in case users want to find out more about what has happened. These collections may include both written material and physical artifacts such as hats and photos. Archives collections preserve the institution's history.

Archives tend to exist within organizations. For example, they preserve records for colleges, businesses, not-for-profit groups, and churches. In each of these institutions they perform a similar function. Newspaper archive departments create archives of their newspapers. Librarians in these departments digitize stories or create microform versions of the paper on film. Librarians also index stories so that users can easily find all previously published stories on a topic. Church archives may collect newsletters, membership information, and property records. A business archive might keep meeting minutes as well as prototypes of different products. In all of these cases, archives can give a user an understanding of the organization in a historical context.

Collections based on geographic location exist, too, such as state or city collections. These archives preserve records of local governments and community happenings. They may preserve local newspapers, property records, or minutes from community meetings. These collections are often open to the local community and provide useful information for researchers interested in a historical view.

Preservation

Of course, when dealing with rare books and local archives, preservation is a priority. If an item is one of a kind—or one of a few—there are not many options to replace it if it gets damaged. Preservation is a complex part of the field that can take a lifetime to completely learn. It involves everything from repairing bindings or replacing pages that have fallen out of books, to disaster preparedness and recovery, to educating fellow staff as to necessary steps to take in the case of an emergency.

Preservation librarians are craftspeople. Their work is a craft that is passed on through apprenticeships and learning from those who have worked in the area for years. This area of librarianship is more physical than others, using a needle or adhesive you work with actual books and materials to repair leather bindings, insert missing pages, and keep materials from decaying. If you have an interest in this aspect of librarianship, you will need specialized training. A few library schools offer courses in this area, and you can often find local classes for continuing education. If you would like to pursue this part of librarianship, a great place to start is an apprenticeship with a conservator, in a library or archive. There are also universities with book conservation training programs that lead to a professional degree.

Digitization

As people come to expect more content to be available online, rare books and special collections have begun to focus more energy on digitizing parts of their collections and putting them online. As most of these collections exist only at the libraries that own them, digitization allows a much broader audience to benefit from the materials.

Digitization is a growing area of librarianship, allowing librarians to meet the needs of users all over the world. Allowing users to access materials online also helps preserve the materials, as researchers do not need to physically handle them. Researchers who just want to read the content can get the information they need without running the risk of damaging the works.

If you are interested in becoming a digitization librarian, you will need to gain an understanding of digitization's best practices and project management methods. You will need to know about emerging cataloging practices associated with digital collections, too. The people working in this area of the field are building a new type of librarianship. By joining this group, you would literally put the library online and make material accessible in entirely new ways.

This type of work, which has grown out of special collections and archives, is spreading throughout the information environment. The *Google Book Search* project is an example of this work on a massive scale. Google currently scans books—not just special and rare ones—to make the books fully searchable, and, copyright permitting, available online. You can see the benefits of scanning rare and archive material in this process, too. Now, people all over the world have access to the books available through this project.

Overall Trends

Rare books, archives, preservation, and digitization let you participate in librarianship with a sense of history, not just because you are working with older materials but also because you participate in librarianship in the most traditional sense. As a rare books librarian, you can learn about a specific collection in a much more intimate way than you can if you are a reference librarian working with a collection of a million volumes. You get to know the materials and work in a highly specialized way, with scholars and researchers who know the subject and are looking to uncover previously undiscovered treasures.

Many people in rare books and archives get to practice librarianship in the largest senses. They may need to catalog unusual materials that do not exist anywhere else. They may work with patrons on highly specialized research issues, providing reference assistance. These librarians have to understand preservation issues in order to keep such a collection safe and sustainable for future scholars. They need to know something about technology in order to understand issues associated with digitization. Knowledge of copyright law is also important as materials are digitized. In preservation and digitization you work to make the documents last longer. Whether you accomplish this through scanning or repairing, the aim is the same: to keep the materials in good condition for use by scholars. In a sense, this is one of the earliest values of librarianship a profession, to preserve information for future users.

In a way, working in rare books and archives gives you the opportunity to practice all aspects of librarianship while working in an area that is constantly evolving and growing with new technologies. Rare books and archives can be a very exciting field of work. You can combine the best of both worlds: the practice of traditional librarianship and helping the field redefine itself through the use of digitization.

Technology

Technology touches every aspect of librarianship. From the move from a physical to an online catalog, to the addition of email and chat-based reference, to ordering books online, to digitizing archives, technology affects every department of the library. Some people say that at some point technology becomes commonplace, and that something is only technology if it is invented after your childhood. For most library staff, many changes have happened within their lifetimes. Many librarians working today remember the introduction of the online catalog, email and chat reference, and the very first electronic resources. So, at present, a lot of these types of services are managed by technology staff. Over time, these projects sometimes move to the department working most closely with them, leaving technology departments to develop programs in whatever comes next. But for now, most people who focus their work in recent developments work in technology departments.

Technology has certainly begun to affect users in their own research strategies. Users tend to think of the Internet first when solving problems, and they rely on *Google* multiple times per day. Some particularly savvy users have used tools like *Google Book Search* or *Google Scholar* and feel that there is little reason to step through the doors of the library for their research needs. However, librarians know that this influx of information means much more information is available to sift through, and that no-one edits the Internet. We help users learn how to navigate today's information environment, judging content for relevance, accuracy, and authority, so we have to know how to get around in this environment ourselves.

This work can be a challenge, but can also be rewarding. It helps position the library for the future and to continue meeting the needs of our users. Technology work is an area of librarianship that can be very exciting if you like to push the boundaries and see where the profession is heading. Many in this part of the field experiment with technology to improve access to information and services. Some experiment with offering new technology-based services. This section will talk about some library technology positions and what each of these roles is responsible for doing in the library.

Systems

Systems librarians design and maintain the library's computer systems. These systems vary from library to library, but nearly always include the integrated library system that runs the catalog, circulation software, and purchasing programs. Systems librarians understand servers, system administration, and library processes. They generate reports, assist in batch processes, and keep databases clean and working. Systems librarians have a specialized skill set. The work systems librarians do impacts most areas of the library, from cataloging to circulation to finding materials in the catalog.

The exact organization of systems work varies by library. Some large libraries might have a systems team, with only a small number of master's degree-holding professionals within it. In small libraries there might be a systems librarian who also is a cataloger or holds other duties.

If this type of work interests you, it would be helpful to cultivate a background in computer science as well as an understanding of database administration. While in library school you might want to gain real-world experience, either through a practicum or a library staff position. It would also be useful to develop a background in networking, Linux, security, data normalization and migration, and scripting. If you aspire to work in a larger library, you might also want to learn about management and training.

Web Design and Applications

As the Internet grows in importance, libraries hire into more positions related to web work. Some of these positions focus entirely on web design. Others are more general positions in which web work is only part of the job. These jobs require knowledge of HTML, JavaScript, database driven websites, web authoring software, style sheets, content management systems, and often include web applications development.

These exciting positions allow for innovation and new directions in library work. If you have an interest in the changing nature of the Internet and making websites that users want to use, this branch of librarianship will be appealing. Important skills in this area of work include understanding good information architecture, design, and the information seeking behaviors of your users. You can learn many of these skills through reading, analyzing web sites, and looking at the institution's website usage statistics to see what improvements or changes are needed.

Some libraries might only have one position devoted to coding. In these libraries, the website would be entirely that person's responsibility. In others, the webmaster works with a number of other librarians, coordinating their contributions to the website. These librarians may be part of a web team, because the library uses a content management system in which any staff member can contribute, or because the webmaster oversees most of the website while subject liaisons create subject guides on their own. Some libraries do not have a person in charge of the website, but instead share duties among library staff.

Web positions require knowledge of Americans with Disabilities Act compliance issues as well as how to design sites that are compatible across a number of browsers. This knowledge helps webmasters create sites that can be used by all people in all computing environments, a consideration of special importance in libraries. To make the most useable and useful sites, webmasters often conduct usability testing and hold focus groups.

This work varies considerably by library size and the priorities of the institution. Some large, research libraries might emphasize their web presence. These libraries can be expected to devote a lot of resources to the program and even have multiple departments focused on the library's website and digital collections. Other, smaller libraries might focus their attention on the physical library and have a relatively minimal online presence. These libraries might only have one staff member who works on the website, and that might be a duty they have in addition to other work.

Technology Training

As technology impacts more of our work, technology training becomes an important way of staying professionally current. Many libraries and library systems have designated staff members whose job is to train other staff members on technology issues. Some of these positions focus on specific tasks in library work such as new circulation systems, online calendaring, or updates to common software. Other training focuses on the new technology our users might use and expect to see in their libraries. Training positions focus on the newest software, tools that the library adopts, or technologies on the horizon.

Some libraries extend training to the library users in addition to library staff. These classes can vary widely; from computer basics to how to use Excel in budgeting to introducing advanced search skills. Technologies change so quickly that it can be challenging to stay current. When a library has a position that holds responsibility for keeping up with new technology and training others, the rest of the staff can feel confident that someone will help them learn what they need to know and help them keep up with their users.

Where Library Technology is Heading

This is an exciting time for library technology. Librarians are witnessing the emergence of open source technology as a viable option for many library services, where they once depended on vendors. Individual librarians are doing interesting things: using blogging software to run a catalog (and allow commenting, adding text message notifications to locate information in the catalog), and using open source content management systems to run the library's website. Libraries are using experimental training programs to keep staff current and make learning about new technology fun.

We also see technology spill over to areas of librarianship that might have seemed unrelated to technology just a few years ago. Hardly a position within a library is completely untouched by technology. Technical services staff use technology in everything from cataloging to purchasing books. Access services relies on technology to facilitate checking out books and running interlibrary loan. Reference makes use of chat services and email reference. Archives, rare books, and preservation digitize their materials to make them available online. Technology facilitates general library work as well. Libraries send surveys in digital formats. Librarians explore ways to use *Facebook* and *MySpace* to reach users who may not typically come to a library.

If you have an interest in technology work, this can be one of the most fulfilling areas of librarianship. You have to continuously learn and adapt, and help your colleagues learn new things. In doing this work you get to help shape the role of libraries within the community and the field. For some, this is the most rewarding aspect of their jobs.

Administration

Library administration does everything from the day-to-day tasks of keeping up with details such as staff time off and facilities issues to big picture duties such as strategic planning and advocating for the library in the larger community. Library administration has responsibility for a range of duties of varying importance, but they all have to happen to keep a library working.

Libraries exist in all sizes. The size and type of the library obviously impacts administrative organization. Library administration can be established in a number of different ways, from one librarian running the organization and performing librarian duties to a director of a large library or system who works with a middle management team. This section will outline library management's administrative duties.

Libraries would not work if not for their administrators. The work they do keeps the library running, and if done well, they position the library to be more effective than ever before. This work can be particularly rewarding for people with a vision for the future of the field and for those who like to help create changes that occur on the local level. If you have a vision for the future direction a library should take, this is the work you should aspire to do. If your library improves, you can share those successes with others in the field in a number of ways, and in doing so you can shape the work that happens on larger levels.

Budgeting

Library administration determines the budget for the organization. They decide how much is spent on the building, materials, electronic resources, new technology needs, salaries, furniture, and anything else the library needs. Often, in large libraries, administration creates an overall budget, passing specific portions of the budget to the heads of the different departments. These budgets might trickle down to individual staff members. For example, a director may determine the total amount of money to allocate towards books, then a collection development librarian may split up the funds by subject, and then a subject specialist may determine how the funds are spent within their subject area.

Working with budgets can be satisfying because you can fund the areas that need strengthening. However, it can be frustrating, because you almost never have as much money to work with as you would like. As an entry-level librarian, you will probably only work with a small portion of the budget, geared towards the subject area for which you purchase books. If you are an administrator in charge of the library, you can only work with the funding budgeted to the library from the community, academic institution, or business.

Fundraising

Many libraries supplement their budget with money from fundraising. Events, book sales, and named rooms are all ways that library administration raises funds within a library setting. Libraries increasingly look for new and innovative ways to create fundraising opportunities. Of course, the type of fundraising varies by the type of library and its relationship to the community.

Many institutions also have "Friends" groups. These groups are comprised of people who enthusiastically support the library. They volunteer, organize events, and implement fundraising programs for their library. Sometimes the Friends group is, in itself, a fundraising organization. In these libraries an administrator might work with the Friends group on fundraising issues.

Some directors in academic institutions work with development officers within the university in order to make sure the university has the right information and targets the right people when doing university level fundraising. This can be particularly helpful if a library, as part of an academic institution, is unable to pursue fundraising goals on its own.

Liaising

Library administration has to advocate for the library when talking with leaders of the community. In academic libraries this could mean the library director advocates for the library to the Provost; in school libraries, librarians advocate for the library to the Principal. In public libraries, the director would need to advocate to the entire community of taxpayers, the local government, and the library board of directors. Library administration needs to be an excellent advocate for the library and their staff, and they need to communicate the needs and interests of the library effectively to power-holders in their community.

Strategic Planning

Most libraries, at some point, undertake strategic planning. This process allows a library to redefine itself and adapt to the changing needs and interests in the community. The administration of some libraries creates this plan on their own. Other library administrations choose to involve the entire library staff in this process. Strategic planning focuses on capturing the direction in which the library wants to go, and documents the specific goals to get to that point. A clear strategic plan helps the administration make decisions about the budget and provides talking points for communicating the value of the institution to the larger community.

Along with strategic planning, library administration is responsible for creating the mission statement of the library and ensuring that everyone knows the primary purpose of the organization. This key declaration doubles as a marketing statement for the community, clarifying the library and its values to their users.

Administrators, of course, have the final say on the library's strategic planning process and decisions. Library administration holds the ultimate responsibility for the library, and, as such, they have to make sure the strategic plan supports the future needs of the library. They also have to advocate and make the case for funding to meet the initiatives that they plan to implement. Creating a plan for the library, receiving funds to initiate the plan, and implementing the plan to completion can be very satisfying for a visionary leader.

Administration Elsewhere in the Library

Finally, in large libraries, there are the administrative tasks that fall to middle management in a large library. This work varies from being involved in important decisions about the future of the library, to participating in large projects like renovations, to the more clerical work of monitoring staff time-off, and paperwork. Middle management often performs staff evaluations and helps work with library staff to develop skills they will need later in their careers.

Management is very rewarding work for many people. You can work with people to and help foster their professional growth. You can help individuals set goals and work with them to make sure they have what they need to achieve them. Team leaders can shape the work of an individual team, which allows you to be close enough to the work of the library that you can still practice librarianship while participating in administration.

Of course, administrative organization varies with the type of library. Larger libraries tend to have more rigid hierarchies and chains of command. This can mean more paperwork and more steps for approval of projects. Smaller libraries may have less hierarchy and bureaucracy, but there can be less opportunity for promotion.

Administrators make the library run and are able to see their visions enacted because of their role within the organization. Though some aspects of the job may not be the most inspirational (fundraising and paperwork come to mind), as a library administrator, you would be in a position where you can think bigger, and in a longer timeframe, and see your vision materialize. If you choose this path, you might even have a role in shaping the future of the field through successes at your library. For many people, that is reason enough to take this direction in library work.

All in One

Many libraries have positions that combine more than one type of position into one role. Medium-sized libraries often have jobs that pull from several types of positions. For example, a librarian might have both technology and reference duties. In small libraries, positions pull responsibilities from all areas of librarianship—particularly if there is only one librarian. Many school libraries and small public libraries may have only one librarian. Some corporate or special libraries have a very small staff. This means that the librarian has to be good at many aspects of librarianship as well as an advocate for their library.

Many solo librarians work with others to achieve the work of the library. A library might have several full time employees without master's degrees, part time employees, or even volunteers. This support staff is necessary for the library to function, but also means solo librarians must split their time between management and their traditional duties. If you like the idea of working with a small collection, running a library early in your career, or learning about all the different facets of library work, this environment could be an ideal fit.

School

As we discussed earlier, many schools have one school librarian, or media specialist. As a solo librarian, a school media specialist might do everything from deciding which books to purchase, to cataloging them, to teaching classes, to providing reference services, to checking materials out. In addition to these traditional library duties, school media specialists may also have to make decisions about the library facilities, negotiate budget issues with the school principal, and work with teachers to integrate library skills and materials into the curriculum.

Librarians in these positions might be the school's technologist as well, helping troubleshoot computer problems, teaching people to use technology, recommending purchase, and leading professional development.

Small Public

Small public libraries, particularly in rural communities, are independent organizations. These libraries focus entirely on the local community, their needs, and their interest. Librarians find themselves doing a little bit of everything, and local people may help with the work. Public librarians in small libraries are in charge of the both collection—selecting, cataloging, circulating materials—and public service—reference, instruction, and programming. A librarian in a small public library may teach the only basic computer classes in a community.

Due to limited resources, these librarians might also have to solicit donations or grants. When public librarians can secure donations to support their work and collections, they create better opportunities for their community. Public librarians who seek grants to support their work need to be able to select good opportunities and write strong proposals in order to make the case that they should get the additional funding.

Small Special

A small special library is often run by a solo librarian, as well. Sometimes they might not even collect many materials, but rather maintain a primarily electronic collection. In these cases the librarians have to negotiate, understand contracts and prices.

Special librarians running small libraries often need to establish on a continuing basis that the library is a valuable use of the organizations funds, perhaps even saving money in the long run. Librarians make this case with data showing that the expenses of running the library are less than the money saved or made as a result of the service.

Solo Overview

Solo librarians are in charge of their library, whether a stand-alone public library or one that is part of a larger organization. If you like doing the work yourself and seeing the payoff of good efforts, this can be an extremely rewarding type of work. With such a breadth of tasks, you can constantly learn and adapt over the course of your career.

New Positions

As libraries evolve and grow in today's information environment, new responsibilities are created and new duties arise that we were not trained to do in library school. For these reasons we see an evolution in the positions available in library job advertisements. These new positions deal with areas of librarianship that might not have been addressed in previous organizational charts.

We hire professional people, possibly with master's degrees in their own subject specialties, to work in libraries and improve our services. Certainly, web development falls in this category. We create positions from other industries, such as marketing, anthropology, human resources and financial development. This can possibly cause some tension between library staff, as these new staff members also have professional status but not as librarians.

Hiring officials face difficult decisions whenever a position opens. If the library loses a cataloger due to retirement or a bibliographer due to moving to a new job, one always has to ask what skill set the library needs the most. Should the new job be a replacement for the old position, or is there a new, more pressing need? Does it make sense to refill the old position exactly, or does it make more sense to reorganize and hire for something entirely new?

Librarians with new positions face the challenging task of carving out their niche, figuring out what exactly their jobs mean to the organization, and teaching others about what their responsibilities include. These jobs can be really rewarding, but they can be stressful, too. This is particularly the case if the institutional culture is not used to their new role. However, if you have an interest in creating a new path and teaching people about how the field is changing, one of these positions might be perfect for you.

Blended Librarians

Many of these new positions fall into a broad category known as Blended Librarians.[10] This concept, defined by Steven J. Bell and John Shank, refers to the idea that many librarian positions combine elements of traditional librarianship as well as the skills of educators and technologists. Bell and Shank suggest that in blending these roles, librarians can do their work more effectively for today's environment.

Librarians in these positions often work directly with faculty and other instructional support staff. These positions are sometimes responsible for designing online learning materials to help students learn to do library research. Other times they work in the reference department to help the department incorporate relevant technology, or they work in technology to help the department incorporate services that would be useful for reference or instruction.

Blended librarians can help show users how the library's traditional and evolving materials and services can help them in their research. Blended librarians can also help libraries adapt through understanding how users approach information. They need to understand technology well enough to know what is possible, suggesting new technology-enhanced services that can realistically be created and offered within their libraries.

---

[10] Bell, S. J., & Shank, J. D. (2007). *Academic Librarianship by Design: A Blended Librarian's Guide to the Tools and Techniques*. Chicago: American Library Association.

Instructional Design

Closely related to blended librarianship is instructional design librarianship. This is a growing area of the field. Libraries interpret this position in a number of ways. The most common interpretation is truly a blended position. In these libraries, instructional design librarians design online learning content. They develop tutorials and guides to using online library resources. They create content to use in virtual reference. They create games to teach information literacy concepts. They use the principles of good instructional design in the realm of online learning.

Other instructional design librarians work on the library's curricula. They help teaching librarians design better instruction, whether one-shot library instruction sessions or semester-long classes. These librarians sometimes train others in education principles and theories and offer professional development sessions to the librarians on good teaching strategies.

Some libraries offer these services beyond the library. They help librarians learn these principles, but train teaching faculty as well. In these cases they open professional development opportunities beyond library staff to teaching faculty, too.

In addition to paying attention to developments within libraries, instructional design librarians also need to stay current in education and instructional design issues, knowing the current topics and trends in these areas.

Information Commons

Libraries are reconsidering how they use their physical spaces. "Information commons" and "learning commons" are physical areas in libraries that are adopted by many academic and public libraries. Information commons provide a one-stop service desk so users can get all their help in one place. Users can ask reference questions, use technology, and check out materials. These locations also often offer productivity software and collaborative space. Users can come to a commons to get access to software, expert staff, and a physical environment for working in groups. Information commons tend to be more open and interactive than traditional spaces in libraries.

This new type of library space requires a new type of librarian to supervise and run it. These positions can fall in a number of places on the organizational chart. They may report to the head of reference, and sometimes report to the library director, supervising the head of reference, circulation supervisor, or other departments offering services there.

Information commons directors tend to hold responsibility for user services training and the user experience. They can be both trainers and managers, training people on library policies and customer service while supervising learning commons staff. They also are responsible for reaching out to the users, marketing the commons and all it offers to the larger community.

User Experience

Another emerging position is one developed to make sure the library pays attention to the experience of its users. Sometimes there are staff positions devoted to this work; other times librarians pick up these duties in addition to their more traditional work. This is such a new and developing part of the field that it is hard to define it clearly for the whole of librarianship.

In some positions, user experience is all about the users. These librarians conduct focus groups and surveys to get a better read on their users, their needs, and expectations. They interview students, use ethnographic research methods, and observe their users in an effort to understand who they are really serving. Using this information, the library can adapt services to what the community has identified as a need or interest. Of course, these librarians are interested in potential users, too, reaching out to the community of members that might not traditionally come through the doors.

Other user experience librarians focus on the online user experience. These librarians have technology skills, know how to code, and spend time designing and creating the library website. They work with users to understand their online behavior and how they respond to the library website and services. They conduct focus groups and do usability testing, and alter their code and web presence based on what the users need.

These positions tend to be experimental, aiming to optimize and expand the user's library experience. Understanding what works well allows the library to replicate success. Understanding what does not work allows the library to re-evaluate the work they are doing.

Finally, user experience positions build relationships with other groups in the community. An academic user experience librarian might form alliances with residence life, campus information technology, admissions, as well as various student groups. In public libraries, these librarians might form relationships with community organizations, arts groups, and government offices.

2.0 Positions

We are witnessing an increase in "librarian 2.0" positions. These librarians understand the social web and how people use it. They understand blogging, wikis, and social software, and how to adapt the library services to make them relevant to users in the web 2.0 environment. These librarians may advocate for chat reference, recommend offering services through text messaging, or create blogs to engage the community.

As newer technologies come along, these librarians evaluate them and determine if they have something to offer their users. If these technologies are deemed useful, they create accounts and begin using the services on behalf of the library. This can give the library a human face, but also can put a library presence in the on-line locations most appropriate for the library's users.

What will come next?

2.0 positions have arisen in the context of today's technologies. Libraries who choose to single out this type of work in one position learn about how new forms of web based collaboration impact library work. As "library 2.0" saturates the field, one can imagine that all positions will begin to contain aspects of this type of work.

There will always be new areas of librarianship that we have not previously considered. Particularly as technology continues to change the information landscape, we will see that libraries have to adapt to new technologies and ways of accessing information. In these cases, we will see new positions created in order to introduce a new idea to the library and help everyone learn the importance and skills associated with the new position. It is hard to imagine what new positions might exist twenty, ten, or even five years in the future!

Many of these positions are new enough that they have not yet been clearly defined. If you work in such a new position, you might be one of a handful in existence. These new jobs do not all have professional groups just for their area of librarianship, as the more established branches of librarianship do. To learn about these emerging branches of librarianship, you have to reach out to find the others doing similar work. Many find this community online. This requires some level of independence, and a willingness to forge one's own path.

It is promising that the field does not feel threatened by changes, but rather adapts by creating these new positions. Libraries today look dramatically different from libraries of the past, not just in the physical layout and collections, but in the way they staff their organizations. These new positions strengthen the library, position them to offer many new services and reach entirely new groups of users, and help redefine the library to meet future needs and interests.

Work in the Library

As you can see, there are a wide variety of positions within libraries. You can hold a traditional library position, work on the cutting edge of library technology service, or balance between the two. Choosing to begin your career in a smaller library will give you the opportunity to try several different parts of library work before choosing an area to specialize in. Taking advantage of short-term positions in library school, such as library practicums and internships, will also give you this opportunity.

In addition to this experience, you can talk to current librarians about the work that they do. Many librarians maintain blogs about their work, and you can read about what they do on a regular day. The references at the end of this chapter provide more sources for information in case you are interested in finding out more about any of these types of positions. Most library schools also offer courses in the different types of library work.

Organizations

Public Service

ALA – Library Instruction Round Table (LIRT)
http://www.ala.org/ala/mgrps/rts/lirt/index.cfm

Reference and User Services Association (RUSA)
http://www.ala.org/ala/mgrps/divs/rusa/index.cfm

Young Adult and Children's Librarianship

Association for Library Service to Children (ALSC)
http://www.ala.org/ala/mgrps/divs/alsc/index.cfm

Young Adult Library Services Association (YALSA)
http://www.ala.org/ala/mgrps/divs/yalsa/yalsa.cfm

Technical Services

Association for Library Collections & Technical Services (ALCTS)
http://www.ala.org/ala/mgrps/divs/alcts/alcts.cfm

Rare Books & Archives

Association for Library Collections & Technical Services – preservation section (ALCTS)
http://www.ala.org/ala/mgrps/divs/alcts/mgrps/pars/index.cfm

Association of College and Research libraries – Rare Books and Manuscripts Section (RBMS)
http://www.rbms.info/

Technology

Library & Information Technology Association (LITA)
http://www.ala.org/ala/mgrps/divs/lita/litahome.cfm

Administration

Library Leadership and Management Association (LLAMA)
http://www.ala.org/ala/mgrps/divs/llama/lama.cfm

Solo Librarians

SLA Solo Librarian's Division
http://www.sla.org/content/community/units/divs/index.cfm

Professional Issues

Librarianship is an exciting field. Librarians learn new things every day. As more information becomes available online, they find ways to incorporate it into existing services or the collection. Librarians resist censorship and protect people's privacy. They also face challenges. The openness of the Internet causes some to question whether libraries should exist. Some want books removed from the shelves, and laws like the PATRIOT Act[11] make protecting patrons' privacy a potential legal issue. Luckily, for times when librarians are challenged by such situations but find it difficult to determine the right course of action, a professional association can provide guidelines.

Like many professions, librarianship has a professional organization, the ALA, which aims to "[t]o provide leadership for the development, promotion and improvement of library and information services and the profession of librarianship in order to enhance learning and ensure access to information for all."[12] All library workers, whether librarians or not, may join the ALA and be active members

---

[11] *Uniting and Strengthening America By Providing Appropriate Tools Required to Intercept and obstruct Terrorism (USA PATRIOT ACT) Act.* (2001). Retrieved October 25, 2008, from http://frwebgate.access.gpo.gov/cgi-bin/getdoc.cgi?dbname=107_cong_public_laws&docid=f:publ056.107.

[12] ALA. *Constitution and Bylaws.* Retrieved October 25, 2008, from http://ala.org/ala/aboutala/governance/constitution/index.cfm.

of the organization. This association will be discussed in more depth in the final chapter of this book.

ALA provides a code of conduct for library staff members. This exists in two main documents. One is the Library Bill of Rights.[13] The Bill of Rights has a role in governing library staff behaviors, providing guidelines for professional conduct. This document advises library staff on ethical matters. In addition to the Library Bill of Rights, which describes the rights of our patrons, the ALA Code of Ethics[14] provides guidance as well. This document codifies the ethical code of the profession.

However, unlike medicine and law, the profession does not sanction or decertify members who do not comply with the association's ethical codes. Though most people who enter librarianship tend to agree with the principles as given, professional are expected to think freely about specific situations and follow the most appropriate actions based on the complete set of circumstances. The association's documents provide guidelines for action and can help guide library staff through complex ethical dilemmas.

A key idea in these documents is that everyone should have free and open access to information. This cornerstone of librarianship can be a controversial one. Some people in

---

[13] ALA. (1996). *Library Bill of Rights*. Retrieved October 25, 2008, from
http://www.ala.org/ala/aboutala/offices/oif/statementspols/state mentsif/librarybillrights.cfm.
[14] ALA. (2008). *Code of Ethics of the ALA*. Retrieved October 25, 2008, from
http://www.ala.org/ala/aboutala/offices/oif/statementspols/state mentsif/librarybillrights.cfm.

the community will always think that libraries should restrict some information. Librarians have to balance the concerns of some members of the community, who may believe passionately that their job is to protect readers, with the general right to read.

This section will elaborate on contemporary issues in librarianship: cultural standards, emerging trends that impact the way librarians think about their work, and areas of activism surrounding librarianship. These topics provide librarians with the opportunity to participate in fascinating professional discussions, which you can join as soon as you are interested in the profession should you choose to become involved with them.

In participating in this extracurricular world, librarians extend themselves beyond their jobs and join the profession. In this sense, to participate in the profession you do not need the degree or a librarian title. Many library support staff members raise some of the most interesting insights into these issues, and many library students begin to make an impact while pursuing their master's degree. If any of these particular areas are of interest to you, you can go ahead and join the debate today.

Librarians and Libraries

When you think of libraries, you may think back to the first library you visited. Maybe you think of the first library where you really had a positive experience. For most people, the library they think of is an actual place. People think of shelves filled with books. They think of the librarian, kindly or severe, and they think of the joy of pulling a book from the shelf and checking it out. Libraries have a strong physical presence, and people have strong feelings for both libraries and librarians.

People tend to have strong opinions about a library's place in society. People like to talk about the physical place in general terms as well as specific stories from their own lives. People like to talk about the positive—and negative—experiences they had in libraries as a child. They like to wonder whether the physical library will need to exist in the near future due to advances in technology. They share their librarian stereotypes and point out all the ways we fulfill or defy them.

To address these strong cultural associations, this section will attempt to briefly discuss the idea of librarians and libraries in society. This background should provide you with a context for thinking about the professional community you are considering joining, as well as to give you a better understanding of library culture in general. As you know, libraries have existed for some time, and in that time they have developed a place in the cultural memory. Even with this prized place, libraries have to navigate changes that challenge and shake up the field from time to time. Understanding librarians and library culture should give you some understanding of how libraries resist and respond to change.

Librarians

First, consider librarians as a group. In choosing librarianship, you will join a profession made up of people who generally love to learn and love information. The first step in becoming a member of this group requires you to earn a master's degree in library studies, so at the least you have to enjoy being a student. Certainly, many librarians love physical books, but a growing number of librarians focus their

their interests on technology and online information. In general, librarians tend to be curious, have a general knowledge about a number of subjects, and have an interest in learning.

Librarians are a helpful bunch, as the profession is built around the values of providing assistance. Though not every position in a library directly works with patrons, librarians all play some role in helping people access information. Archivists preserve it. Catalogers make sure you can find it. Reference librarians help people find the answers to their questions. Access services staff help people get the materials they need. The helpfulness that the profession generally extends to users can also be found within the professional community.

As librarians tend to be helpful, the field welcomes newcomers. If you have questions about the field, your job, or how to check in at a conference, you will find someone willing to help you with your question. People do not join the field if they do not like assisting others. Librarianship should not be too daunting to newcomers. Students can take advantage of many opportunities to get involved and there are mentoring programs if you spend a little time looking for them.[15]

Internal stereotyping might surprise you as you enter the field. Sometimes people make sweeping generalizations about different parts of the profession, such as reference librarians or catalogers, or the difference between people who have been in the field for some time and those who are new to it. You will hear about a host of librarian stereotypes even as you begin your degree. You should remember that just as

---

[15] The references for further reading at the end of Chapter 5 have a list of resources for people new to the profession.

general stereotypes of librarianship are not particularly helpful for the field, internal stereotypes sometimes have a negative impact, too.

Outside the library profession, you will probably hear jokes about glasses, buns, and an obsession with cats. People think of a quiet, shushing librarian who sits behind a big desk. Librarians have been portrayed in various roles from the librarian *Party Girl* to *Batman* to *The Mummy*. Real life librarians react to these portrayals in different ways, from pride to indifference. Though you might have mixed feelings about these stereotypes, you can find solace in the fact that these cultural references clearly show that librarians have made an impression on people over the years. As the saying goes: any press is better than no press.

Library Organization

We have talked in previous sections about library staff members who lack the master's degree in library studies. Without these staff members the library could not function. They are often the first line of interaction for patrons, answering questions, referring patrons to a librarian, or checking out their materials. They may perform a more basic level of cataloging or teach some technology classes.

These staff members are referred to as para-professionals, or in some cases, support staff. Perhaps the best phrase for this group is "library staff." Some libraries involve these staff members in major decisions and they go to their own professional development training. There are conferences for these workers and organizations designed to support their specific needs. They can also join the ALA.

However, many of these positions do not pay as well, and some of the work tends to be routine. To be promoted to librarian's status, in most cases, you have to have the degree. If you have a desire to impact the direction of your institution, it makes sense to pursue your master's degree. Many people find a job as a library support staff member while working on their degree. Some libraries will provide funding to help staff members earn a master's. Others will offer exchange or flex time to help employees balance work time with classes. Many libraries will give employees the opportunity to try out some of the skills they develop while working on the degree. Even where that support is not provided, students will see the benefit of their coursework on the job, and will see how their library work will inform their academic life. If you pursue a Master of Library Studies degree, it will certainly benefit both you and your institution in the long run. Your work experience will also benefit your classmates in your program as well, as you will be able to explain how the curriculum ties to day-to-day library work.

Some academic libraries have faculty status for librarians, creating yet another hierarchical division within the library. This also changes the organization of the library. Faculty status typically provides librarians, as a group, more access to decision-making and a more transparent way of running the organization. This also adds further hierarchy to the library, creating levels of rank for librarians in addition to the existing hierarchy that exists between library staff and librarians. Many libraries with faculty status require librarians to serve a set number of years before applying for a promotion. This means that you may not progress up the ladder as quickly as you could in non-faculty organizations, even if you achieve outstanding work. However, the benefits of faculty status can make this trade off an acceptable one for many.

Libraries

Even as many Americans read less than in the past, many people still fondly think about libraries. People who like to learn and read can understand the magic of being in a place full of information and books, and they love libraries because of it.

People tend to think affectionately of the library as a place. Some people think of majestic Carnegie buildings and others may think of the cozy library with nooks for reading that they grew up visiting. Some immediately think of large research libraries while others think of their local branch. People have diverse images of libraries, though they are generally positive. This positive image secures their place in our society, granting them an important space in our cultural memory. Some people think so highly of libraries that they even get married in them!

As information has moved online, many libraries have taken their services there, too. Often, the types and number of services offered online depends on the library's community and its resources. Once a library offers services in this new way, it has to work to educate its users about the new approach and market it to their community. When libraries offer services online, and the community is aware of this and makes use of those services, librarians help build on their community's existing image of libraries. Libraries today can offer relevant services and information online as well as a positive physical presence.

Library as Place

Many librarians are thinking about a concept of "library as place." They turn to this at a time when people talk about finding everything in the nebulous world of the Internet. Research on the Internet does not require a specific location or time of day, but the library is very much rooted in the real world. For this reason, libraries explore community building and what role they can play as a physical place.

Some libraries create meeting spaces for students to study together or for meetings of community groups. Others create programs around areas of local interest. A book club may meet to discuss books by a local author, or people may come in to take a class on local history. In these cases librarians and library staff focus on the value they offer their community and build spaces and programming around it.

Focusing on the concept of the library as a place gives the library a clear sense of its reason to exist and gives the community a clear reason to maintain funding. Coffee shops, information commons, children's play areas, and meeting rooms are all clear indicators of a library's consideration of its role in the community and its view of itself as a place for people to gather.

The library as a place creates an open community space where people can come together to work as a group or share information. Libraries exist for their communities, and physical libraries provide services for people who are located nearby. Whether the community is transitory, as students typically are, or a more stable basis of support, as found in many cities and towns, these communities come to a library for a common purpose: to learn, share, and find new information and ideas.

Libraries are currently in a challenging position within society. They are highly valued by many, yet others may question the value of their existence. Despite these challenges, there is clearly a need, and a place, for libraries within society. Different libraries meet different needs, and each community has its own set of requirements and interests. It is just a matter of determining the needs of the community, evaluating how the library is situated to fill it.

Librarianship offers us an exciting and meaningful area in which to work. Helping people find information, or teaching them to navigate today's information environment, is extremely rewarding. Libraries provide services and information to people no matter their standing or position within society. Some people are only able to access the Internet through their local libraries. Other community members may have access to rich information resources on their own but not know to sift through it and evaluate it. The library can help in a range of cases, from providing resources that some may be unable to access on their own to teaching users how to evaluate the sources they have found.

Librarians have to understand the new forms that information takes and the best ways to make this new information findable and usable. The librarian focused on digital preservation of information shapes people's understanding of librarians and the role of libraries in society just as much as the librarian leading a local book group does in their community. All of these jobs are important to the field and shape how people understand what librarians do.

As most people have used libraries at one point or another, they often feel qualified to debate the future of libraries and librarians. You should realize that if you choose librarianship as a career, you will be called on to participate in these debates and that you will represent the field as a whole for some of your friends, acquaintances and family members.

Libraries in Communities

Libraries are a cornerstone of democracy. In a time when information was scarce, libraries gathered, preserved, and provided access to news and information about the world. By pooling the resources of the community, the library became a place that could afford to purchase a broad array of expensive or hard-to-get resources, and could share them back to the community.

Libraries offer information to everyone, regardless of their standing in society. They provide a place of education for those who are not part of an educational institution and they help provide access to information to people who might not otherwise be able to access it. Libraries promote literacy and learning in their communities. This community component of librarianship draws many people to the field. It is a noble profession, about helping the improve itself. Librarianship shares this goal with educators and people who work in community service professions. For many people, this work is more appealing and ethically congruent with their worldview than work that is directed primarily toward financial gain.

The impact of the library on the immediate community, whether it is a geographic area, school, university, or business, is made through the work of the librarians and library staff. In the services they provide, in their collections, and through their cataloging, librarians and library staff make a difference in the quality of the community's life or work. A strong library can lead to a strong and well-educated community.

For this reason, librarians should always approach their work with the question: how can the library best meet the needs of its users? Whenever librarians approach any problem in the library they should aim to think about what their users need most, and how the library is uniquely positioned to meet those needs.

This also means that libraries are exceptionally focused on customer service. Where profit might motivate businesses to cater to customers, librarians are motivated by a desire to serve the community. Creating a positive customer service experience will encourage users to return to the library and make use of its resources and services again in the future.

The Role of the Library in Communities

The library, more than many organizations, has to understand what goes on in the community. Librarians have to know what community needs or interests are on the horizon, what the reading interests and information needs are, and the ways in which the local community prefers to access information. They have to know which way the political winds blow and what their future budgets might include or lack. They have to understand who the primary users of the library are as well as know which segments of the population are not yet using the library. The better the understanding of the community, the better job the library can do at providing good information, materials, and services to their users.

Libraries operate within systems and they have to understand the entire organization in order to know how to offer the best possible services and to plan for their future. Knowing the total system allows librarians to know what they need to do, what support they will get to do their work, and where they can help to lead their community into the future. Libraries act as both members of the local community and as outsiders, evaluating the community's need objectively.

Access to Information

Libraries provide a very important service, collecting information for community use. In some cases, they do this through purchasing an expensive resource, like an encyclopedia, that individuals may not be able to afford on their own. In other cases the library collects many quality resources on a topic so that people learning about something new do not have to research and purchase materials themselves.

In some cases, a librarian helps users learn to locate information on their own. In others, they may teach patrons to evaluate information for accuracy. Librarians can help users to both understand which resources are good as well as how to evaluate any source that they find.

A large part of access to information is collection development. Librarians think about the information needs the community has and seek out the best materials to fill them. Information could be practical, such as how to build a porch, or it could be scholarly, like postmodern critiques of Shakespeare. A special library may fill more specific needs, such as finding legal rules and regulations for a law firm or medical research for a pharmaceutical company.

Training

Librarians offer a number of types of training for the community. They can help people learn to do research based on the questions that are asked at the desk. They may conduct training sessions in areas where people have expressed interest, such as genealogy or using a specific database. They sometimes create training programs in various new technologies or might create credit-based classes.

Librarians offer instruction on a wide variety of topics to a diverse group of patrons. As with any aspect of library work, the key thing is to know the needs and interests of their users in order to tailor instruction to them. Training sessions sometimes take place in the library and sometimes take place elsewhere in the community. For example, a librarian might teach a library instruction class on history research in the history building, or a children's librarian might go to a local elementary school as part of an outreach program.

Training programs vary by type of library. School libraries teach children the very basics of research, the way the library is organized, and how to pick out good reading materials. Academic librarians aim to teach skills for searching in specific databases to find scholarly articles, or how to use bibliographic citation software, or the critical evaluation of information. Public libraries sometimes focus on technologies or specific types of research based on local interests.

Individual instruction is also quite common to library work, no matter the type of library. Many librarians find this type of instruction particularly rewarding. These one-on-one sessions provide librarians the opportunity to target the interests and needs of a specific user, allowing the librarian to see the difference instruction can make. As a librarian, if you develop a relationship with the patron you can help them develop higher levels of research skills over time.

Literacy

Libraries advocate for literacy in communities. They offer early literacy programs, such as story hour for small children, and they offer tutoring for young people and adults who cannot read at their desired level. Through offering reading material of any type, libraries facilitate people's literacy and encourage regular reading.

Even the most frivolous of books offers users a chance to practice the skill of reading and improve their ability. Libraries offer fiction books as well as nonfiction works, so that users have the opportunity to rad for pleasure as well as find information. Even academic libraries offer pleasure reading to attempt to instill a life-long love of reading in young people.

It is important to keep the language needs of your community in mind. For example, if you have a population of patrons that primarily speaks Spanish, you should offer reading materials to support this group. Certainly, a small demographic should not require major additions to your collection, but libraries ought to make sure they do not neglect some of their users or potential users when providing materials to support literacy.

Digital Divide

Most libraries offer some information through online databases or access to the Internet. Librarians or other library staff may provide computer instruction so that patrons can use these resources. This is particularly important and useful in public libraries. Libraries offering these services help bridge the digital divide. The concept of "digital divide" relates to access to technology. Sometimes the phase focuses on economic access to technology tools and the Internet. Sometimes the phrase describes generational trends in differences relating to technology skill. Other times, the phrase explains the phenomenon of easy access to broadband in urban areas, and slower access to the Internet in more rural areas. No matter how one interprets the phase, it always describes unequal access to technology.

Libraries are positioned to help mitigate against the effects of the divide. They offer computers to those who do not have access, and training to those who might lack the experience. A vast world of information is available to people with the right skills and access to the tools. For that reason, librarians, as professionals interested in providing information, have an interest in providing access to information technology.

Of course, technology is expensive, and the skill sets associated with current technology change fairly rapidly. Providing current technology requires significant resources from the library. To stay current, a library has not only to purchase recent technology, but provide training for staff members. This can challenge libraries with limited resources. In these cases, libraries can seek grants that provide funding in order to provide the tools, and there are some scholarships and an increasing array of free training opportunities for those wishing to enhance their technology skills.

A Gathering Space

As we discussed in the section on "library as place," libraries often provide a physical gathering space in the community. They offer a place for people to meet and collaborate. They provide places for story hours and reading materials for children, and can be a safe environment for teenagers to hang out and experiencing their shared culture. When libraries are gathering spaces, they provide a cohesive public space for the community. A library in this role creates a place where anyone in the community can be part of something together. This service can be as important for the community as the access to information.

Libraries go about creating this space in different ways. Various changes can be made to a library to create useful community spaces, from the modest improvement of making the stacks more appealing to the more obvious change of adding a coffee shop to the building. Libraries that already have good gathering spaces might host events to bring people into the building. Events that get community members to come through the door will help them to understand this aspect of the library's role. Many libraries now offer a combination of quiet and collaborative spaces so that users can find a place regardless of their personal preferences. Some libraries create small conference rooms so that groups can meet and discuss things without bothering others.

Libraries work to fill gaps in the community, reaching the needs that people have, providing access to information, and providing the training that they need. Librarians must have a strong understanding of the community—their interests and needs—and an understanding of what the library can offer the community.

Librarians can gain this knowledge through active participation in the community, conducting surveys and focus groups, and getting to know their users personally. By paying attention to the users and trying to get to know the people who never consider coming to the library, librarians will have a better understanding of the community as a whole and the library's role within it. Armed with this knowledge, librarians can make better decisions about the best way to use the community's resources: the best materials to purchase and lease, the most appropriate technology to provide for the community, and the best roles for staff members within the library.

Above all else, librarians do what they do to help their communities. The first step is to pay attention to the community's needs and interests, and to think carefully about what libraries do and why they do it.

Intellectual Freedom and Intellectual Property

Intellectual freedom is a topic near to most librarians' hearts. It is a core area of interest for the ALA, and there are several ways to get involved in activism around this issue if you are interested in it. Intellectual freedom is so central to librarianship and what librarians do as a profession that the ALA has an Office of Intellectual Freedom as well as a roundtable on the subject and several subcommittees dealing with related issues.

As important as it is, most people are not aware of the concept of "intellectual freedom" until they have spent a little while in the field. Intellectual freedom is a broad term with a number of different aspects, but fundamentally, it refers to the right that everyone has to seek and receive information. This means all information, even if it is unpopular or counter to a community's way of thinking.[16] This chapter will address several facets of intellectual freedom. Many people's first thought of intellectual freedom relates to censorship of books. Today, the issue of censorship applies to the Internet as well, and concerns the use of filters in some libraries and educational systems.

Intellectual property is a related topic. Intellectual property (copyright, patents, trademark, and trade secrets) defines the type of property that is essentially in the realm of ideas rather than physical things. Intellectual property includes what one writes, composes, or creates. Unlike with physical property, the theft of creative content does not remove it from the creator's possession. When someone photocopies a book, but it does mean that the author loses the potential to profit from a sale. Since libraries collect out copyrighted works or provide access to them via the Internet, libraries deal with intellectual property in most everything that they do.

Censorship

One topic of particular importance to librarians is censorship. Librarians, generally, have a strong interest in keeping materials available for the community and will fight against

---

[16] This right is so important that Article 19 of the Universal Declaration of Human Rights addresses the issue, stating, "Everyone has the right to freedom of opinion and expression; this right includes freedom to hold opinions without interference and to seek, receive and impart information and ideas through any media regardless of frontiers." http://www.un.org/Overview/rights.html

censorship whenever possible. Librarians celebrate Banned Books Week to raise awareness about censorship, and will encourage people to seek out books that have been previously banned. Librarians intentionally buy controversial books, saying that a library's shelves should hold something that offends everyone. This is not as literal as you might first expect. Librarians do not seek out controversy, but they try not to avoid it either.

Of course, librarians also use professional judgment and consider other factors. Controversial materials are inappropriate in some environments. A special library might have only scientific data, and something that would be interpreted as controversial should not necessarily be part of the collection. A library catering to children should not have books on every adult topic.

With such strong feelings about censorship, it is also worth noting that librarians often walk a fine line in the very work they do to build their collections. When a librarian chooses not to purchase a specific title, the book or journal is not available to the users. Librarians have to ask themselves if they avoid getting a book or resource because it is not right for the collection or if they are avoiding controversy. If the major hesitation is that the title would be controversial, then you would have to ask, "Why not purchase it?"

Internet Filters

Internet filters are very controversial in libraries. Some libraries are required to install them because a source of funding requires it or because of a law. Some libraries receive grants that require the library to use filters to continue funding. In these cases, if your library does not use a filter, your library will not receive money. In other cases, state or federal lawmakers have required the use of filters in public agencies. Most of the time, filters are not installed in libraries by choice, but rather because a rule requires it.

The argument for filters, in most cases, is about children accessing inappropriate information. People know how easily one can find unpleasant things online, and worry about children's early exposure to sex and violence. In most cases libraries do not supervise computer use, so eliminating access to questionable content is a process that has to be automated.

However, most filters work based on a keyword system, and not human eyes. Filters are imperfect, sometimes letting through the objectionable content that the filters are intended to block. Other times it keeps perfectly valid information from the user because of an unfortunate choice of words. Sometimes popular sites like *MySpace* are blocked entirely. This is a source of controversy, as it implies a value judgment about the website.

Perhaps the most frustrating things about filters, from the library point of view, is that they can block important and valuable information. If a student researches breast cancer they could miss valuable sources because the websites they need to access include the word "breast" or medical images. Likewise, regardless of what one thinks about *MySpace*, a sociology student could find relevant research material there. If computers automatically filter the websites, the user will not get the information they need.

Copyright and Loaning Materials

Libraries are able to share books because of something called the "first sale doctrine."[17] This doctrine allows people to share materials that they have already purchased. It also allows a student to sell his books back to the bookstore at the end of the semester. Libraries have pay attention to copyright laws to continue functioning in an effective way.

Many academic libraries offer electronic reserves, or e-reserves. E-reserves offer materials that professors would like students to read but are not included in the required textbooks. To offer these materials, the library scans in an article or section of a book and makes it available online to students enrolled in a class. From time to time, this sharing of scanned electronic materials is determined to be a borderline copyright violation.

Many rules surround movies, and one rule that impacts many organizations is that they cannot show movies in a public setting without paying a fee. Some libraries circulate DVD's or videocassettes, which is allowed, but copyright law does not allow public showings unless the library purchases performance rights.

The digitization projects that are so exciting can only be applied to certain materials. If the library owns the copyright or negotiates with the copyright holder, as may be the case for materials developed by the institution or for personal works given to the institution by community members,

---

[17] U. S. Copyright Office. Subject Matter and Scope of Copyright. In *Copyright Law of the United States of America*. Retrieved October 25, 2008, from http://www.copyright.gov/title17/92chap1.html#109.

or if the work has fallen out of copyright and into the public domain, the library can digitize the collection. Libraries have to be careful when digitizing materials to make sure they only do so when it is legal.

New Copyright Models

Some librarians advocate for new models of copyright in order to improve people's access to information. The Open Access publishing model[18] is one example. As part of this movement many academic libraries are developing institutional repositories. To contribute information to a repository, one has to own the copyright to the material in question and must not have given up publication rights in a contract. This is often not the case after publishing a work in a journal or through a publisher. Librarians make an effort to educate the university community about intellectual property ownership so that people can keep their copyright after publication and add their content to the institutional repository.

Another, sometimes related, copyright model is the "Creative Commons" model proposed by Lawrence Lessig.[19] In this model, people choose the level of sharing they wish to grant for their own copyrighted work. People can keep all of their rights under their copyright, let anyone use their materials with citation, or only allow people to use the material as long as any derivative works are not for profit.

---

[18] This is discussed in greater detail in the next section on institutional repositories.

[19] *Creative Commons*. (2008). Retrieved October 25, 2008, from http://creativecommons.org/.

Creative Commons licenses also let content creators choose whether the works may be modified by others.

Librarians need to pay attention to copyright and the emerging world of alternative models to be able to best advise users on how to use the materials they find. Photos released under the Creative Commons, for example, can enhance a report or presentation. However, to make use of these materials a user has to know about their existence, know how to find them, and understand the required citation.

Librarians are passionate about intellectual freedom and pay close attention to intellectual property. These issues are intimately tied to the practice and profession of librarianship, and knowledge of the current state of these issues helps librarians be more effective.

Intellectual freedom cuts to the core of what libraries do. Librarians provide access to all types of information for all people. They help people find the information they require in order to learn what they need to know. If librarians are limited in their ability to do this because of censorship or Internet filters, the functioning of libraries is compromised.

Likewise, to advise people on the legal use of information, librarians have to understand copyright, the rules for the use of various forms of intellectual property, and how they might be able to use various materials in the future. Intellectual property rules are constantly being negotiated. The Internet and digital content continues to challenge everyone's understanding of copyright, the rules for which were created for a print world. Digital media shapes how people expect to use information and the ways that people do their work. Some industries, like the music and film industries, respond by advancing more restrictive interpretations of copyright. Others, like some independent musicians and visual artists, use the open nature of the Internet to gain more fans and build a larger base of customers.

This area of the field is quickly changing and impacts a number of specialties within librarianship. The better you understand what is happening in the realm of intellectual property, the better you will be able to advocate for the needs of libraries.

Technology

As technology grows in importance in society, librarianship sees changes occurring both internally and externally. Some colleagues want to offer new services and tools for their users. Some patrons have increasing expectations for technology integration in the library. As this book has discussed, technology impacts librarians' work in a number of ways. Technology allows librarians to make library materials available digitally, but it also causes some to question the need for libraries. Many people entering library school today will inevitably encounter someone questioning their wisdom, wondering why you would get a graduate degree for a field that they assume will not be around in ten years. However, what you learn in library school and what you experience working in a library will give you plenty to say about the future of librarianship.

If you enjoy the Internet and other technologies, this can be a very exciting part of the field. Technology work lets you forge the future of the field and experiment with new tools and services that the library can provide. Librarians experiment with reinventing libraries and are working to help people see the added value librarians provide in this information-rich environment. If you have an interest in strategic planning, trend projection, or simply are dedicated to libraries' continued existence, technology will give you a voice in this discussion.

Many people assume that to work in a technology field, you must know how to write computer code. Certainly, to do certain jobs and to make some changes to a website, this is true. However, technology is not just about writing code. A growing area of technology work deals with the user and studying how users interact with information. This work can happen in the graphic design of websites, usability testing, and conducting focus groups. To participate in this work, you have to know enough about technology to know what questions to ask and to have enough technical background to be able to communicate with the coding staff. Just having basic background can be very helpful, but it is important to be able to remove yourself from the technology enough to speak in lay terms when working with users.

Digital Repositories

Some libraries, particularly those within academic and research institutions, are exploring the concept of creating digital repositories. In doing this, libraries create online environments for scholars to store their work. This work can be material they have produced for a peer-reviewed journal, assuming the copyright agreement allows for it, or other scholarly materials they have developed, such as white papers or departmental publications.

Digital repositories signify the entrance of librarians into the field of publishing. They look more like traditional bibliographic databases than anything else, but they represent a new way of thinking about publishing and spreading knowledge. This is still a new area of the field, with many people creating the systems that other libraries will use in the future.

A library that develops an institutional repository has to develop an online database. Librarians have to figure out preservation, cataloging and access issues, as well as the technical back-end. This combines the traditional skills of librarianship with well as some level of technical and coding aptitude.

Online Presence

When libraries create institutional repositories they help shape how people expect to interact with library information. Libraries offer collections online, answer reference questions through chat, or make their catalogs browse-able anywhere. When a library offers information online, users can happen upon the information, even if they did not know the library offered it. If you can make your library's website rise to the top of a Google search, you will find that your collection is seen more often and by more people.

Putting the catalog and databases online extends the library to the researchers, wherever they are. When libraries and educators first began putting content online, the aim was to meet the needs of users who were not physically nearby. However, over time, librarians found that everyone wanted access to online material, even if they were physically located within the building. Today, this type of access fits with users' lifestyles. Sometimes libraries purchase online materials from vendors so that they can offer this type of information. In addition to these out-of-the-box solutions, librarians also look for ways that they can create additional opportunities for an online presence.

Certainly, digitization is a good example of extending the library's online presence. Once material is digitized it can be contributed to several sites in addition to the library website. This makes it more available, and when the material is hosted on a number of sites you can have the content link back to your homepage.

Librarians have learned from this process and look for new and innovative ways to extend their services online, too. Librarians routinely use chat reference to interact with patrons, and many libraries offer online tutorials. Some experimental librarians have created *MySpace* or *Facebook* pages in order to reach patrons in yet another environment, and to help put a human face on the library.

Library 2.0

In this vein, many librarians are paying close attention to Web 2.0 and looking for ways to adapt their work in light of this evolution in the online world. The first Internet, in retrospect sometimes thought of as "Web 1.0," was a read-only environment. Most people could only read the content. In order to contribute you had to be a bit of a geek. You had to know how to write basic HTML and get your content on the Internet. Web 2.0 is for everybody. You can think of it as more of a read/write environment. You can certainly still access web site content as if in the early days of the Internet, reading what is there. The change that comes with Web 2.0 hinges on the idea that you can also write information, even without coding knowledge. On many sites you can simply create an account, click edit, and write.

This shift in the Internet has impacted a wide variety of fields and ways of doing things. Expectations are changing in light of this. Many organizations are becoming more transparent and user focused by paying attention to recent developments online. Often the lessons of Library 2.0 are things librarians have known for a long time: customers are important; it is a good idea for the library to have a human face; transparency is a good thing; listening to your community is important. Though these ideas have been around for some time, for some, the online world reinforces and strengthens the message.

This way of thinking has impacted librarianship mostly through the Library 2.0 movement. Library 2.0 has been somewhat controversial, as some have questioned whether it really is any different from how libraries have always operated. However, Library 2.0 did evolve out of this way of approaching the Internet. The original discussions advocated that users should have the ability to share information, leave comments, customize their library profile, and make use of a number of Web 2.0 trends when they interact with the library website.

Since this original, technology focused conception of Library 2.0, librarians have evolved in their interpretation of the movement, and are now much more focused on the user experience. Today Library 2.0 is as much about communicating openly with patrons, asking to hear more suggestions from them, and providing a space for conversation as it is about the technology tools. Library 2.0 is shifting to be more about finding out what the users want by engaging them in conversation, changing the layout of the library to be more open and collaborative, and relaxing policies so that the library does not seem too stodgy to be much use to today's users.

Technology in Libraries

Libraries often provide technology tools to users, as well. The specific technologies that libraries offer vary by library type and community, but the concept of loaning technology is similar to loaning books and other materials. In lending out devices or computers, libraries make an expensive resource available to a community that may not have the ability to access it on their own. In pooling resources all parties have access to more information.

Some libraries simply offer computers with minimal office software and a connection to the Internet. Others check out equipment to users, from e-book readers to digital cameras. Some have sophisticated software or hardware that stays in the library building, but the library provides space on a networked drive, training, and the ability to work on a given project over a long period of time.

Experimental

As technology continually changes, and staying current typically requires an investment in order to keep up with the newest gadgets, some libraries experiment on behalf of their users. Some purchase and circulate iPods with audio books on them. Others circulate e-book readers so that users can see what it is like to read on a paperless device. In this way, the library invests in the newest technology, and gives their users the ability to try out different tools before investing their own funds.

In general, technology is an experimental area of library work. New tools and services come out every day. Being new, there is no definition about how this technology might help users or the library. Technology staff members work to understand the possible technological impacts by getting experience, looking for ways the new technologies can improve services and workflow, and recommending whether the library should adopt it or not.

Sometimes new technologies make sense and fit with library work. For example, though some people may have assumed that libraries only purchase and circulate books, movies were a logical addition. Ordering, receiving, and circulating movies mirrors what libraries have always done with books. People might have an easier time understanding the library's investment in e-books, but that type of material is different enough from traditional books that libraries have to rethink ordering, receiving, and circulation in order to provide them.

Some experimental work is not about what libraries loan at all. It focuses on the way libraries offer their services or the way they represent themselves on the web and in the community. Some libraries offer "roving reference," a service that looks a lot like what clerks do in stores. Roving reference librarians approach patrons who look like they could use help. Sometimes these librarians carry technology around with them to make it easier to help the user on the spot.

Some librarians take reference out of the building, holding office hours in a coffee shop or in their academic department. In these cases they may even take useful books to show users what to look for when they visit the library. Most certainly, these librarians have a laptop computer so that they can show users how to navigate the website and how to log in to use the online resources.

In many ways technology enables librarians to be more experimental. The tools allow libraries to think differently about what they do and the ways they meet their users' needs. Sometimes that act of experimentation alone allows librarians to re-evaluate their current practices and make their services better.

Technology is an exciting and rapidly evolving part of the field. If you like change and innovation, work in this area can be extremely rewarding. You can see the impact of your work and help colleagues adapt to generational and cultural changes.

It is also an unpredictable part of the field. It is nearly impossible to guess what things will look like in a year, much less in ten. Technology changes rapidly, and some library users change rapidly with it. Librarians need to understand these changes in order to know the best ways to adapt their services and remain relevant in their communities.

Technology work, today more than ever, does not require that you be proficient at coding or a certified geek. It just requires that you look at emerging technologies and that you know who your users are. If you keep these two factors in mind, you will have a clear sense of what to do with the new technologies. It is simply a matter of keeping a balance between trying new things and staying reliable enough that your current patrons will recognize your library and what you are doing.

Advocacy

Libraries need advocates. As libraries face continuing challenges in the field, they need people who can clearly articulate their strengths and values to the community. Librarians and library workers can be advocates, library friends groups and Board of Trustees can be advocates, and library users can be advocates, too. Sometimes advocacy simply consists of making sure that people know what the library offers. Other times advocacy means pursuing funding from local government or from donors.

Whatever the advocate's relationship to the library, library workers need to support them. They need to make sure that the people who speak out in the support of libraries have what they need in order to make the most effective case. Librarians need to work with their advocates to make sure they know the needs of the library and the reason for the requests.

Marketing

One method of advocacy is library marketing. Librarians need to market their collections and services in a way that reaches all of their potential users. Some advertise in local media. Some advertise through government programs. Some libraries create objects, like t-shirts or coffee mugs, with the library logo. Marketing can also take place through programming. Good programs, advertised in other community spaces, can help bring people into the library.

Some marketing has been extremely effective. For example, most people know the ALA "Read" posters when they see them. These are the posters with famous people holding either a book they wrote or a favorite book to read. These posters have become part of the culture, and help people remember libraries and what they do.

Academic libraries may use library instruction sessions in order to share the numerous services offered within the library and on the website. A public library may have an informational booth at a local festival, themed to the topic of the festival and showing relevant resources.

ALA Advocacy

One of the ALA's main purposes is to be an advocate for libraries and librarians. In addition to the "Read" posters, the organization coordinates marketing messages such as the "@ your library" campaign. These campaigns allow libraries to coordinate their messages to make sure they are consistent enough to be recognized across the country. This gives the strength of the organization to local libraries and a way to tie the messages together on a larger scale.

Day-to-day

Librarians' day-to-day work is a form of advocacy. Every good interaction with a patron, every helpful answer given, and every time a child learns to love reading, someone learns about the positive work that happens in libraries. These patrons go on to advocate for libraries in the future. In doing their jobs, and doing them well, librarians practice advocacy for libraries and librarianship.

Advocacy is one of the more important things that librarians do. Librarians do good work. It is important to make sure that the community knows what libraries offer them. In reaching more users, libraries have more people who will advocate for them. And in an era when technology causes some to question the very place and role of libraries, libraries need as many people speaking out for them as possible, from paid employees to users.

Luckily, through ALA, advocacy for libraries is a coordinated effort. If you need talking points, ALA can probably provide them for you. There are a number of services designed to make it easy to advocate for libraries. Taking advantage of these services will help maintain the library's status in the community.

Issues in Librarianship

Librarianship as a profession is motivated by its shared professional values. Librarians make decisions by thinking about what is best for the community as well as turning to the profession's value statements such as the Library Bill of Rights or the Code of Ethics for the ALA. When faced with censorship, privacy, or preservation decisions, these are the lenses through which librarians make decisions.

At the same time, people wonder what libraries will be like in the future. The broader information environment is changing, and it is clear that libraries have to adapt in some ways. Some librarians focus on the value added through traditional library skills and services. Others focus on ways that libraries can adopt and adapt to using new technologies. Many blend the two, focusing on continuing the work that librarians do best while also adapting in other areas.

Understanding these general trends in librarianship will help you understand the issues that you might face once in the profession. Knowing the services that the ALA offers, understanding the profession's ethical statements, and having a familiarity with new technologies will help you face future changes and understand the way libraries can adapt to new situations.

Getting the MLS

At this point you might have realized that you are interested in librarianship. Congratulations! It is a great field, and you will find continuous challenges and opportunities to learn. You will be able to contribute to your community and make it a little better than it was before.

To get to the place where you are able to become a librarian, you will need to get a master's degree in library and information studies. This program can be as short as a year, or as long as you can stay in a program. You can enroll as a full-time student or work full time and take classes part time. Some of these programs are very academic, requiring a thesis and comprehensive exams, and some are focused on practical applications of library studies, requiring a capstone project instead.

This section of the book will focus on finding programs, the application process, and tips for making the most of the program. If you approach the process strategically you can make sure to have an experience that will position you well for your future career. It is important to think about this; there are many new graduates in library studies every year, and practical work experience can make you more competitive once you are looking for positions.

When looking into programs you will want to consider a number of factors. You will want to think about the quality of program as well as its specialty. You will want to consider which library schools are nearby, whether you are willing to move to attend one, or whether you want to pursue a distance degree. You will need to make sure that the program is accredited by the ALA, as most positions require that your degree to have that accreditation. You will want to look at the required coursework to make sure it covers what you want to know, and you will want to look at the electives to make sure you can learn the other things you would want to learn. It makes good sense to see who the professors are in the program in order to know who you might study with, and try to meet some students or graduates of the program to see what they think of their experience.

Once you know the programs you would like to apply to, you will want to prepare an application. Most applications are completed online at this point, and include standard information such as an application form, undergraduate transcripts, GRE scores, recommendations, an essay, and a resume. If you are nervous about the application process, it is worth keeping in mind that this is a professional degree rather than a strictly academic program. If you have relevant work experience, whether working with customers in retail or managing files in a medical office, you should explain how this relates to the fundamentals of librarianship in your application.

Getting into a program is just the first step. Once you are in a program you will want to take advantage of the many opportunities for learning and professional involvement available to you. As a student you can get discounts on professional memberships, which means you can get all the benefits of membership, including publications and participation in discussion lists. Students can often get reduced rates and scholarships for conferences as well, providing them a window onto the profession and the opportunity to meet working librarians in a variety of libraries and positions. You can participate in internships or practicums, which are short-duration jobs at libraries, to get experience in a variety of jobs, in order to get a better sense of what it is

you would like to do when you graduate. You can participate in discussion lists, blogs, and online networks through
sites like *Facebook* or *Twitter*. It is important to remember that
master's degree programs in library studies are professional
programs rather strictly academic programs. It is wise to
become part of the field, to begin establishing yourself, and
to look at your possible futures during the time you spend
pursuing your master's degree.

The time you spend in graduate school preparing for a
career as a librarian can be a very exciting time. At that
point you are still new enough to the field that you can explore a variety of types of work without committing to one
area. You can ask simple questions, and no one will think
anything of it. You can get started writing and presenting on
things you study in school, to see if it is something you enjoy. Library school is like librarianship with training wheels.
You can choose to pursue the degree with a lot of enthusiasm, or you can put minimal effort into the degree and
graduate. However, you should realize that the more effort
you put in early on in your career, the more likely it is that
you will be able to find the position you want once you
graduate.

Finding Programs

So you know you want to be a librarian. After reading
this far in the book you are interested and excited about the
field. You have an undergraduate degree and you are willing to work to get experience while in library school so that
you will be competitive when you graduate. What do you
do next?

First, you need to find a graduate program.

To be a librarian in most libraries, you need an ALA accredited master's degree in library studies. This can be called many things: Master of Arts in Library Studies, Master of Library Science, Master of Library Studies, Master of Library and Information Studies, or a Master of Library and Information Science. For some school media jobs you will not need an accredited degree, though you should be confident in that path as you may not be able to change careers later to a library position requiring the master's degree.

ALA Accreditation

ALA accreditation is granted by the American Library Association. To be accredited, a library school has to prove that it meets their qualifications. This accreditation is only for a given period of time, after which the school has to apply to renew its accreditation. The accreditation process involves paperwork, meeting with current students, faculty, and alumni, and a final decision-making meeting at the Annual ALA conference. Some schools are granted provisional accreditation, with a shorter time period until renewal and an expectation of improvement.

ALA accreditation is granted to schools within the United States and Canada. Whether you earn your degree in Canada or the United States (Puerto Rico included), as long as it is accredited, you will be able to work in a library.

Distance

A few accredited programs are offered online. These programs might include some classes where most or all of the work is done at a distance, using the computer. This can be particularly helpful for people unable to move to pursue the degree, or for those who wish to continue working in their present job while taking classes.

Many people question whether these degrees are as good as traditional, in-person degrees. However, the very act of earning a degree online proves that you have a basic level of computer literacy. In librarianship, this can be a very useful skill to have. As more and more library users expect to get some of their service online, this experience gives the student a unique window into the users' experience and can help the library understand how to adapt their services and information to be more relevant to people comfortable with the online world.

Coursework

Just like in college, library programs include a set of basic, core classes. These vary by program, but they typically include courses that deal with an introduction to the field, reference, cataloging, management, and technology. Beyond the core of a program, students can take electives in areas of interest, such as children's literature or academic librarianship, in order to gain the most appropriate background for their chosen fields.

You also will probably need to choose a track. Most of the time library programs offer academic, school, public, special, and perhaps technology tracks. Students take courses within these tracks, positioning themselves for a specific area of librarianship when they graduate. It is wise, even if you know the area you want to work in, to get the basic qualifications for as many types of libraries as possible. This way you will be most flexible when you graduate, and will have broader-based knowledge of the profession.

Some library schools require a master's paper or thesis to graduate. Some have comprehensive exams. Some have a capstone project that you must complete. Find out about this early on. If you know that you will need to write a long and thorough paper, you can tailor your coursework to prepare you for that project. If you have to create a portfolio of the work you accomplished as a student, you will want to keep your coursework from the day you started the program.

Field of Study

It is important to consider the types of classes available in a given program when considering where to enroll. You should think about the types of jobs you might be interested in pursuing and what skills you would need to learn to be able to do them. Once you know the skills you would need, look at the curriculum of a program to see if it would meet your needs. For example, if you are interested in preservation, but you do not see many course offerings in this area, it is worth talking with someone in the school about your area of interest. A faculty member will be able to tell you whether they will offer the courses you want in the next few years, whether there are opportunities for workshops in your area, and whether there are alumni who have graduated and gone into your chosen field.

Professors

When considering whether a school will meet your academic needs, you should also find out about the professors teaching and doing research at the institution. If you are extremely interested in systems librarianship, and there are no systems librarians or programmers on the faculty, there is a chance that you would not get the education you would want to be part of the field.

Professors can also prove to be valuable connections in the field once you graduate. Do the professors know the movers and shakers in your area of librarianship? Will they be able to connect you with practicums in your area of interest? Could you go to them for advice about practical questions once you are working in the profession?

Having an idea about the professional background and research interests of your potential faculty will help you understand how they will prepare you for your future as a librarian. You know the types of opportunities that would be available to you at a specific program and which professors will give you professional advice.

Talking to Graduates

One great way to get to know whether a school is appropriate for your areas of interest is to talk to the graduates. You can often get a list of willing alumni from the library school, but you might want to ask around on your own, too, to get reviews from people who did not enthusiastically sign up for an ambassador program.

You can ask alumni about their experiences in the program and about things they wish they had known when they were in school. You can ask about their professional careers and how their education has given them the tools for achieving their goals. You can also ask about what they have heard from colleagues elsewhere. Alumni know their school's curriculum, and can help you understand whether the program will meet your needs and expectations. They can also help you get a sense of the preparation you will gain and where the program might lead you.

Ask Around

Of course, not everyone knows a pool of librarians that they can ask for insights about a program. Unfortunately, you need information the most when you know the fewest people.

Luckily, there are a number of resources for people who want to find out more about the field and specific programs. There are a few listservs for people new to the field. People regularly discuss their library programs and give other potential librarians pointers. This is an excellent place to listen to the conversation and ask questions while you are looking at library schools.

Librarians also tend to be an open group. If you are excited about the field, you will easily find people to talk to. You can even ask the librarian at a reference desk. It would be a highly unusual question, and the librarian at the reference desk would most likely enjoy talking about the opportunities of librarianship.

You may know librarians, as well, or you can pick a random library's on-line chat reference service to get more information. This can also be particularly useful if you are looking to go out of state for library school. Look for the academic library at that institution, and you will probably be able to find someone who can answer your questions about the library school. This way of finding out about programs can be particularly useful if you are looking at programs across the country, but are unable to travel to look at every school you are considering.

Geography

Librarianship is not like law; you do not study librarianship for a particular region, nor do you have to practice in the state in which you earned your degree. You do, however, begin forming your network of colleagues while in school, and this network is the one that you will probably end up relying on to some extent when looking for positions. A practicum in one library will allow you to meet several people. These people are part of the local network and can serve as excellent references when you are looking for a position. So, although you are not necessarily bound to stay in the same state in which you earn your degree, it might be easier to find employment there.

Of course, our profession is not limited to a single region, so you might decide to move. Some states have several library schools, so even if you make many contacts while you are a student it might be difficult to find a position because of the high population of library school graduates. If you participate in email discussion lists, online communication forums, or attend conferences, you will begin to build a national network of colleagues.

Your library school will be your introduction to the field. There, you will get to know the core concepts. You will meet professors doing research in the field and you will make friends with the students who will be your future colleagues. You will get the opportunity to participate in practicums or internships, getting your first real library experience and meeting practicing librarians. As a student you can get discounts for professional association memberships and discounts for conferences.

Choosing a program gives you a foundation for your future as in librarianship. This program will be a gateway to the larger profession and the beginning of your professional network. It is an exciting and big decision, one that will set your career in motion.

Preparing for Programs

Once you have found the programs that appeal to you, it is time to apply. The process is a relatively simple one, and is similar at most schools. This section will explain a little about the process and some tips and techniques for your applications.

First and foremost, you should spend time looking at the website for the school you are interested in attending. There should be clear guidelines there for what you need to include in your packet and a little bit of information about the type of application they are looking to receive.

Armed with this information, you should be set to begin pulling together your application packet. If you have questions along the way, you should feel comfortable asking the administrative assistant or professors in your potential program for clarification. For the most part, however, the process should be pretty simple.

Relevant Education

When creating an application packet, you will need to include your academic transcripts. These will tell the program about your prior work as a student. In addition to your transcripts you will most likely need to write an essay about your interest in libraries and your plans for your professional career. Your academic experience has likely given you talking points on this very issue.

The application process will give you the opportunity to evaluate your education and experience up now. You would be wise to consider how your education has prepared you for both graduate school and the field. Think about your coursework. In addition to the information you learned, what was your library experience like? What types of research did you do? What materials are you familiar with? What library services were particularly useful for you? Your life as a library user gives you plenty of relevant experience when thinking about libraries and talking about your understanding of the field.

You can also think of your college major. Chances are that if you majored in a liberal arts field you have lots of library experience. You will probably have a lot in common with most librarians. However, you are likely to have some library experience no matter your area of specialization thanks to general education courses. Even if you majored in the hard sciences and spent more time in the lab than in the library, your experience as a library user is a relevant perspective, and added to this you will have a subject specialty that may be relatively uncommon in the profession at large.

One of the nice things about librarianship is that it is a field of generalists. On a staff of seventeen people, every person might have a background in a different subject. This gives a multitude of perspectives and a strong network of people to go to if you have a question outside of your area of expertise. Someone specializing in interpersonal communication might collect for all of communication or even the social sciences; collection areas are broad. You might be able to collect in your favorite subject, or one that is just out of your comfort zone. If you have a background in an un-

usual area, you will probably be given that area with enthusiasm.

Relevant Experience

You will also probably need to submit a résumé with your
application packet. Like the transcripts, this gives the library
school an understanding of who you are. In this case, you
are helping them understand you professionally. You should
include any relevant work that you have done, even if it did
not take place in a library.

Even if you are applying to library school straight out of
your undergraduate career, you probably have work experience that is relevant and should be discussed. Remember,
the library school is evaluating your application both on
your academic background and likelihood of success as a
graduate student as well as the likelihood that you will go on
to be a successful librarian. We have already clarified that
you have relevant experience as a library user, just having
graduated from college and completed research assignments
as part of your requirements for graduation. You should
definitely also include relevant work experience in your application.

If you have ever worked in retail or at a restaurant you
have a wonderful customer service background. Working in
these environments gives you a surprising amount of relevant experience and numerous interactions with customers.
You can refer to specific examples of how you have dealt
with difficult people, how you have made the customer experience better for your clients, and your customer experience philosophy.

Other types of work experience are equally relevant. Office work often involves filing, management of office infor-

mation, and providing service through the phone like telephone reference. Drawing analogies between what you have done and library work can be helpful for the selection committee. If you would like more information about library work in order to make more effective comparisons, you should ask a librarian. And if you have ever volunteered in a library, or held a student job, that information is relevant to the library school as well. The main point is to think about how your experience could relate to library work, and to include that on your resume and in your essays if that is applicable.

Grades

The weight placed on grades varies by school. If you are concerned about your grades, you can ask the school if they can give you the average GPA of entering students. Another option you have is to consult Peterson's Guide to Graduate Schools. In the Library Science section you can find information about the program and compare yourself to other students. It should be noted that as a professional school, library schools often do not require the high GPAs that some academic fields require, and may give greater weight to other aspects of your total application package.

That being said, the better your grades, the better your chance at getting into library school. If you are concerned about your chances, you should work to keep the highest GPA that you can earn. This will also allow you to position yourself better for potential scholarships to help pay for library school.

GRE

The GRE (Graduate Record Examination) is to graduate school as the SAT is to college. Most colleges require a score on the standardized exam as part of your application, but some only ask for it as an optional item in your packet. The general version of this exam has three sections: language, math, and writing, and it will be quite familiar to those who have taken the SAT. One of the main differences is that it is offered on the computer and the online test is adaptive. If you answer a question correctly, you get a slightly more difficult one. Answer a question incorrectly, and you get an easier one. This continues until the exam can find your average level of successful question, scoring you based on that level. If you are concerned about the test, there are plenty of study guides available. There are practice tests online and courses if you are willing to pay for them.

Essays

You will likely need to complete a series of essays as a part of your application to library school. The specific prompts or questions will depend on the schools you are applying to, but some typical ones are about your personal views and goals. You might be asked to write a personal statement or a library philosophy. Take this seriously, but do not be too worried about stating everything precisely as you will as a practicing professional. You are applying to library school in order to learn about the field and to get a better understanding of it. One would hope that by the time you graduate your views will have changed!

You might be asked to write an essay on why you are considering librarianship as a career. This is an excellent place to talk about your reasons, draw on your experiences that show you will excel, and make the case that you are prepared, motivated, and know what you're doing.

Recommendations

Recommendations are a good place to showcase both your strengths as a student and your potential as a librarian. You can go to your best professors, the ones who can speak most clearly to your qualifications, and get them to write about you as a student and researcher.

You can go to former employers and ask for them to write about you as an employee. In these cases it is wise to ask for a recommendation from someone who has had some graduate school experience so that they know what they are recommending you for. It is most important, thought, to get a recommendation from someone who can speak to your enthusiasm, skills, talents, and ability to work well; such a person will be your advocate.

If you know any of your former librarians well, you could also approach them for a recommendation. A librarian may know the program you are applying to, will know what it takes to be successful in the field, and will be able to speak to your potential in both arenas.

Most schools will have a requirement or a recommendation about how many of your former professors must provide recommendations. It is wise to follow their advice and get the number of recommendations they request, or more.

Résumé

When completing your résumé, your goal to sell yourself as a librarian. You will want to think critically about the experiences you have had and couch them in terms of how they will make you be a better librarian.

The experience of preparing a resume will be a useful one. You will be making résumés, or their more complicated cousins, the curriculum vitae, for the rest of your career—any time you apply for a job or special program. Getting used to thinking about all of your experience and applying it to a specific type of work is an extremely important skill. As you look at the entirety of your experience look for ways to tie it to librarianship you will discover how general skills relate to specific librarian positions.

One strategy for learning the language of librarianship and understanding what to include on your résumé is to look at current librarians' resumes to see what they say and describe. If you know any librarians personally, you can ask them if they are willing to share their résumés. Another option is to look online for librarian résumés or curriculum vitaes. You will find a number of them. This gives you an understanding of the skills that are valued in the profession, the organization of professional résumés, and whether you are looking in the area in which you would like to work. It will also give you an understanding of the length and format. Academic positions, for example, tend to require a longer format, while public libraries require a shorter résumé.

If you are applying to library school right out of college you might not have very much work experience to cite on your résumé. That is okay. Think carefully about jobs and student organization experiences that might be relevant. If you were a president of a campus club, that shows leadership. Leadership skills are useful no matter what field you are going into. If you organized events, you can talk about that as a type of project management experience.

Application Packet

Once you have completed your application, you might be tempted to send it off immediately and get it out of your hands. It is wise to wait if you have completed it before the deadline. Take a day or two to let it sit it on your desk and not think about it. Come back to it with fresh eyes and read over everything. Does it make the points you were hoping to make? Are there any errors or grammar problems that did not get caught in the first round of proofreading? Do you have everything required in the packet?

If you still have time, you might want to have a few people look over it and see if they have any recommendations or see any holes in your application. Your references might be a good choice for this, presumably, since they already know you and are working to help you get accepted. You probably want both your facts checked and the grammar and details looked at by multiple eyes. This is good practice; you will want to do this when you submit applications for library positions in just a few years, as well.

Of course, if you are completing your packet near the deadline, or if the school has a rolling deadline and you are applying close to the end of their process, you might want to submit it as soon as possible to ensure that it reaches the school on time. It is still a good idea to get the details checked, though, so if you have friends who could look it over quickly, it would be helpful.

Tips to Keep in Mind

The process of applying to graduate school is a lot like library school itself. It is an experience that is helping prepare you for the field of librarianship. The processes of reflecting on your experience and finding ways to tie it to a position that you are interested in is something you will always need to do when applying for positions. You will always need to find people who are willing to serve as recommendations for you, accurately judging whether they will be able to speak to your strengths and represent you well. You will always have to write something when applying for a job. It might not be an essay as graduate school requires, but you will be writing cover letters explaining your background, philosophy, and the way you meet the job requirements, which is a lot like the personal statement that is required in an application to a master's program.

You will always want to look over all of your materials critically to make sure they are accurate and correct. Job searches require an exacting eye for details in grammar and the way you present yourself. You will always want to have at least a second set of eyes look over your application materials.

After all of this, you are evaluated for a specific position, and granted entry or not. The position you are applying for is as a graduate student. It is worth noting that library schools are not gatekeepers to the profession. They accept people primarily on their ability to succeed in graduate school. They also want their students to succeed and represent them well in the field, so they undoubtedly look at their ability to succeed after school, but that is not their primary responsibility. A master's degree in library studies is not a pass to the profession, so once accepted you will still need to work to make yourself competitive in the job market.

While in School

This book is about deciding whether librarianship is right for you and kicking off your career with that all-important qualification, the master's degree in library studies. However, from day one it might be useful to be looking ahead to how to make the most of your time in school, as it will go by very quickly. This section is designed to help you think about what you can be doing while in library school to be as competitive as possible once you graduate. Our field is one where there are jobs, but it is often hard to get exactly the job you want in exactly the location you want in the pay range you desire. The more competitive you are the better your chances at getting exactly the position you hope to get.

Master's Degree as a Professional Program

The first thing to know about the master's program in library science is that it is a professional one. You will be entering graduate school, but the program is not like the academic programs that some of your friends might be entering. This difference is not a negative one, but rather a distinction between types of programs. While academic programs might focus on theory and original research, professional programs focus on preparing you to join a profession. At times you will either be thrilled that you do not have to worry about all the theoretical information, or you will wish that you had more theory to support what you are learning to do.

Academic graduate programs train people to be scholars. You learn the language of your field, the way academics interact with each other, the type of research accepted by the community, and the way that people get information within a discipline. Library school teaches you to be a librarian. You similarly learn about the scholarly work and dissemination of information through the field, but you also learn about the practice of librarianship. You are being trained in how to be a member of that community, and as such it makes sense to go ahead and get involved. As a student, you have access to many different tools and networks, and some are easier to get involved with as a student than as a new professional.

Internships/Practicums

Internships and practicums are extremely useful. They are a great opportunity to get real world experience for a short period of time. You can try out different jobs and different types of libraries. While doing so you can build up your professional network and get to know other people in the field. This is a time when it is okay to ask any question at all. Forget what "OPAC" stands for? It is a safe time to ask.

Email Discussion Lists

Though you will undoubtedly be a busy graduate student, you will have pockets of time that you can fill with library discussion lists. There are lists on nearly every topic imaginable within librarianship, and many are for members of the ALA. A simple search for your topic of interest will return many options. You can subscribe to these lists just to read what people are saying. You can learn a lot through lurking without saying anything that would impact your reputation in the field. It is worth keeping in mind that

many of these lists' archives are available online and if an
employer looks for you in the future they might be able to
turn up something you said in one of these environments.

Literature and Professional Writing

There are so many sources of library literature and writing today that it can be hard to keep up with it all. Generally there are three main categories of materials: journals,
trade publications, and blogs.

Journals are the scholarly format that librarians teach
students to use every day. There are a number of these in
the field, some of which librarians contribute to, some of
which library school faculty write for. Many of these include
articles by both. These articles tend to be well researched
and scholarly in nature. They might explain the results of
original research or give a current state of a branch of the
field.

Trade publications contain current news in the field, case
studies, and informative articles with far fewer citations.
These tend to be quick to read. Many of these come with
membership to the ALA and its subgroups.

Blogs and wikis are a growing area of importance. Many
librarians are contributing valuable information about their
work in these types of publications long before the information can make its way into a magazine or journal. You can
read up-to-the minute information about how a library is
implementing a new service, and share opinions about library news.

You can also publish as a student. There are journals specifically for students. There are writing contests. You can
start your own blog. The student perspective is a valuable
one, and many people are interested in the state of library

school education. You are in a unique position to report on that part of the field, the same way you might choose to report on the area you plan to work on at graduation.

Online Networks

In addition to blogging there are many online networks you can join. These, of course, change with technology, so it is hard to anticipate which ones might be popular even six months in the future. *Facebook* has several networks for librarians, and many libraries use *Twitter* and *Friendfeed*, too. If you are interested in technology at all you might want to consider playing in the new communication technology arenas as they arise. Many new online networks operate as free, open chat rooms or as email discussion lists that never close down.

Of course, if you are not as focused on technology, you should not feel pressure to join every new network that comes up. However, you should know that people do find online places to connect across distances. Some ALA groups use *Facebook* groups to connect. Some working groups use *Google Docs* to collaborate across distances.

Professional Organizations

Join professional organizations while you are a student. Memberships are at their cheapest when you are in graduate school. For this reason, you should consider joining any organizations that you think you might ever possibly be interested in while still a student. This way you can see which ones provide useful information, which ones seem to be most useful to you, and which ones you would like to work with. Then, post-graduation, you can cancel memberships in the ones that did not meet your in the ones that did not meet your expectations and focus your energy on the organizations most useful to you.

Of course, the main organization to consider is the ALA. This is the premiere organization for the field and one that most library staff belong to. Within ALA there are several groups based on type of library, issues of interest, or job type, as well as numerous committees. There are many niches within the ALA, so if you want to get to know what is going on in these different areas, it is worth looking at sub-groups.

There are many regional professional organizations as well. This can be a good way to get to know local people in the field, attend professional meetings with lower travel costs, and get to know the current issues in the local library community. Because these organizations are smaller, they might have fewer events and publications, but they might have more opportunities for enthusiastic library students to get involved.

There are also several free organizations to get involved with. For example, you could join the Blended Librarian community. They are entirely online and deal with the intersection of education, technology, and librarianship. They have an active discussion forum and host periodic free webcasts. The Librarian Society of the World is a loosely formed group of librarians who use technology to communicate about forward thinking issues. If you are interested in something, you can either find or create your own free network of library professionals using many of the free tools available today.

You might think that as a student there is not much you can do to get involved beyond attending conferences or meetings, but, actually, there are many ways to get into being an active participant in the field. Getting this experience while a student is very valuable. It shows initiative and proves that you will be capable of being professionally active once in the field. Many committees are always looking for the perspective of a student, or new member of the field, so sometimes you can actually use your status as a student or a new librarian as a way to get involved. In some ways, it can be easier to get involved as a student than as a first year librarian.

Getting involved in librarianship is really as easy to do as being prepared and willing. If you step forward, volunteer to do something, and follow through with your promise, people know you to be reliable and will think of you for future opportunities. You can do this on a local level, in virtual communities, and even on the national level.

Conferences

Students often get good rates for attending conferences, and there are a number of funding opportunities for those who are interested in attending but who do not have funds. Sometimes students can get further reduced rates for volunteering to serve at the conference. At many conferences you can also often get conference registration fees waived if you present a paper, though not at ALA conferences.

Attending a conference as a student gives you the opportunity to try out anything that looks interesting to you. Once you have a job you might only choose to attend programs that are related to your position. As a student you might attend a program aimed at instruction librarians in the morning, something on children's literature in the afternoon, and a cataloging program in the evening, all as a way to find out more about the field.

Attending conferences is often another way to get involved in committee work. ALA and local committees are always looking for interested people. By showing up in a meeting, paying attention, and volunteering your services if there are any opportunities, you are opening the door for committee participation in the future.

Finally, you are able to meet a lot of people, possibly including well-known experts in the field. You should feel free to introduce yourself as a student when you meet new people; they might have tips and recommendations regarding things to see or do at the conference and may even provide tips for jobs later in the future.

Conferences can also be a way to get to know librarians. Once you start attending a specific conference regularly, you might start seeing the same faces year after year. You get to know these people and look forward to seeing them at each conference. These people become part of your social circle and your professional network in case you want to collaborate in the future or need advice about a project.

Leadership Programs

Many state organizations, groups based on professional affiliation, and even the ALA offer leadership programs. Some are fairly competitive; others just require a registration fee. Some have specific aims, such as teaching about the organizational structure of an association, while others focus on general leadership skills.

Leadership training does not end when you are early in your career, so it is not something that you have to feel like you have to do early or never at all. However, there are many opportunities for people just out of library school.

There are also a number of fellowships available once you graduate. These positions tend to last for a year or two, and give you the opportunity to learn about a diverse array of library work within an institution, often giving you access to mentors and library leaders.

Job Sites

It is a good idea to monitor job-related websites while you are in school. Watching job sites will help you understand what types of positions are commonly available, the skills that people are looking for in different positions, and the vocabulary that employers use when describing their jobs. Once you have an idea of the skills that different libraries are looking for, you can make sure to take classes that help you learn what you need to know. Understanding the required experience will help you tailor your internships and practicums to what you know you will need when you graduate. Knowing how often the positions come up that you are interested in will help you understand how challenging or easy it will be to get the job you want.

Summary

Working on a master's can be an exciting time. You can be introduced to a number of different parts of the field and try on different types of work in different library settings. You can join various associations for less that you can as a professional, getting to learn about different types of cutting edge work, you can try out different conferences, getting to know the types of work that you might be able to do.

Certainly, some people complete the degree requirements, graduate, and go on to library work. Others pursue
every opportunity available, trying to have a fuller understanding of the field and get the most experience possible.
No matter your path, you will learn more about librarianship and have a better idea about what role you would like
to play within the field.

Further Information

Oh the Places You Will Go

http://www.ala.org/ala/educationcareers/careers/librar
ycareerssite/ohtheplaces.cfm
ALA's site for potential librarians.

ALA Accredited Programs

Directory of Programs:
http://www.ala.org/ala/educationcareers/education/acc
reditedprograms/directory/index.cfm
This directory will allow you to search for programs in a
number of ways. The site includes a printable PDF, a
browsable Google map, and a searchable database.

Guidelines for Choosing a Program:
http://www.ala.org/ala/educationcareers/education/acc
reditedprograms/guidelinesforchoosing/index.cfm
ALA has released this list of guidelines for selecting an
accredited master's degree in library studies.

Frequently Asked Questions:
http://www.ala.org/ala/educationcareers/education/acc
reditedprograms/faq/index.cfm
Many questions you might have about accreditation are
included here. This page gives a brief explanation of what
it means to be accredited, things students should consider,
and discusses some general issues around the MLS degree.

General Financial Assistance Information:
http://ala.org/ala/educationcareers/education/financial
assistance/index.cfm
This page contains a directory of awards from local, state,
national, and foundations for study in library and information studies.

ALA Scholarship Program Information:
http://www.ala.org/ala/educationcareers/education/sch
olarships/index.cfm
This page contains information specifically about financial aid from ALA.

Information about Jobs

Articles about Library Jobs
http://www.liscareer.com/
LIScareer offers a number of articles on a variety of career issues. Many aim to address issues for people new to
the field.

ALA Job List
http://joblist.ala.org/
ALA brings together a number of jobs under one search
interface.

General Library Jobs
http://www.lisjobs.com/
This search allows you to browse positions in a number of
ways.

Library Day in the Life
http://librarydayinthelife.pbwiki.com/
In 2008 several librarians chronicled the work they did
during a day or week of their work. This sites links to participants' blogs. Using this site you can see what library
work is really like for people in a wide variety of positions
working in a wide variety of library settings.

Library Society of the World
http://thelsw.org/
The Library Society of the World is an informal group of
librarians who communicate online. It is included in this
list as an example of how librarians are using the Internet
to form groups around various areas of interest. The Library Society of the World tends to be more technology
focused, and they use a wide variety of emerging tools to
maintain communication with each other throughout the
day.

Library Success Wiki
http://www.libsuccess.org
The Library Success Wiki contains information about
what other libraries are doing. You can see which librar-

ies have implemented a specific service and how. You can use this site to get an understanding of library best practices, the adoption of new tools, and the libraries that are doing cutting edge work.

Online Professional Development

Blended Librarian
http://blendedlibrarian.org/
The Blended Librarian community consists of a discussion board and regular, free webcasts. Topics tend to focus on issues related to librarianship, education, technology, and design.

Online Programming for All Libraries (OPAL)
http://www.opal-online.org/
OPAL offers free, interactive webcasts on a variety of topics. You can access archived programs at http://www.opal-online.org/archive.htm.

SirsiDynix Institute
http://www.sirsidynixinstitute.com/
SirsiDynix offers regular webcasts dealing with technology and career issues. You can subscribe to these free webcasts and download the podcast after the presentation has been given. You can access the archive at http://www.sirsidynixinstitute.com/archive.php.

Webjunction
http://www.webjunction.org/
Webjunction is an online community provided by OCLC. This community allows you to friend other librarians as

you might in *Facebook* and provides access to a number of professional development opportunities.

Blog Search

LISZen
http://liszen.com/
LISZen allows you to search only library blogs for information of interest.

Librarian Blogs and Sites Directory
http://librariansindex.blogspot.com/
This site contains an alphabetical list of librarian blogs and websites.

Library Weblogs
http://www.libdex.com/weblogs.html
A list of library weblogs by geography.

Conclusion

At this point you should have a pretty good idea about librarianship as a field. You know about the different types of places that librarians work, the variety of jobs that librarians do, some of the current issues of the field, and how you can get started in library school. You probably have a feeling about the type of library that you would enjoy working in the most. You may know that you want to work with young adults, college students, in a public service component, or somewhere with minimal public interaction. You probably even have some remarks ready in case someone asks you about the future of libraries and you may have plan for how you will get to library school and what you will do once you are there.

Does this all sound too perfect? To be clear, any profession has its issues, and librarianship has its own set of challenges. This section will address some of the current challenges in the field so that you have an even perspective.

Possible Challenges

Occasionally, email discussion groups for new librarians will lament that admissions to library school come easier than professional positions once you graduate. The master's degree in library studies does not guarantee a job when you graduate; it just provides you the entry-level requirement. Library school admissions offices are not in the business of choosing the next generation of librarians; they are in the business of selecting people who will succeed in a graduate program in library studies. While in library school, a paraprofessional position, internship, practicum, or even volunteer work can supplement your coursework and give you experiences that will help you stand out when you apply for a professional position. Combining real world experience with academic coursework will set you ahead of those who only have the master's degree.

Depending on your location and job of interest, the field may provide challenges for finding your first job. An anecdotal saying often shared with library school students says that you can have any two of the following: the job of your choice, the location you prefer, or the salary you would like to earn. Some people find all three, right out of school. Some have a harder time and can just find a position fitting just one of their preferences. Some people, to break into the field, take any job they can get in order to add more experience to their resume. If you are a competitive candidate, you should be able to find a position that offers at least two of the three goals. Once you have more experience, and you have gained greater credentials, you will have an easier time finding a position that meets all three.

If you already imagine yourself as a library director, note that moving into management positions within libraries can be just as challenging as moving into management in the business world. As in any field, options diminish as you move up the professional ladder. However, you can often find positions that allow some level of management work right out of library school. The library degree often includes a management course with the understanding that entry-level librarian positions are really mid-level library positions. New librarians might manage volunteers, students, or support staff, and may have responsibility for decisions and budgets within their departments. However, note that moving into middle management positions can require moving to a new organization.

The financial health of libraries might concern you, too. As with many not-for-profit organizations, budgets are getting tighter. Shrinking budgets can influence the daily work of library staff. Some libraries face a stagnant collection of resources, or lack the capability to upgrade their technology as often as they would like. Sometimes open positions go unfilled or are reclassified so that they no longer require a master's degree or pay a librarian's salary. This can mean that work shifts throughout the organization, changing what individuals do on a day-to-day basis. You should pay attention to the health of the libraries in the geographic area that you choose to work. Some libraries have strong budgets and support, but some face significant challenges.

The same shrinking budgets can also impact your professional development opportunities once you are in the field. Less funding can mean that you are able to go to fewer conferences or workshops, or that you have to pay for some of these opportunities out of your own pocket. Some librarians find that these experiences have enough professional value that they pay their own way to go to them. Others do not find them as useful or do not have the flexibility in their personal budget to cover their expenses. Institutions in this position might find that their staff members have varying levels of skills and current knowledge. If you believe that professional development opportunities are important, you should ask about these opportunities in job interviews, as many institutions make this type of funding a priority. You can also take advantage of a number of free or low-cost learning opportunities that are available today online or as part of the local library association.

Despite the associated challenges, librarianship is a great field. Any profession that you might consider working in will have its own strengths and weaknesses. The question regarding librarianship, as with any field, is whether the positives outweigh the negatives. Does the fact that the work is varied and interesting and can provide you with an opportunity to keep learning outweigh the fact that it might be harder to get your foot in the door? Or would you like to help children learn to love reading so much that you can possibly forgo professional development funding?

Information Science

But let us say that you start your degree and decide that it is not all that you had hoped. Perhaps you decide that you do not really want to work in a library, or you decide to look outside the field. Maybe you graduate and decide that none of the available jobs look particularly interesting. The work that you put into preparing for librarianship can still help you professionally, even if you choose another path. The background for librarianship also prepares people to work in occupations outside the field.

The master's degree in library studies essentially focuses on information. It centers on how to organize information and how to find it. It describes how to do good research. These skills are increasingly important in a number of fields as information becomes more readily available. When finding information is exceptionally easy, it becomes more important to have someone who can navigate the information environment, distill a large body of information into a smaller pool of the most relevant information, and to vet the information that an organization uses to make decisions.

People who do this type of work are working in the area of librarianship and information science, even if their job title does not say it. People do this work in businesses, news agencies, and in market research.

The Profession of Librarianship

The coursework for the library degree covers topics traditionally associated with librarianship, but can also address a number of other relevant areas of knowledge. You might take courses in educational technology, usability, and computer programming while you also take traditional classes in reference or cataloging. These courses could prepare you for other paths if you decide you would rather not pursue librarianship for your entire career. They may open up opportunities for consulting and part-time work. The courses you take help you grow as a librarian, allowing you to bridge your library work with other areas that your library would like to develop.

Though many librarians also have a background that opens doors outside librarianship, many people who hold a master's degree in library studies feel strongly connected to the field. Getting the degree, working with librarians, and becoming professionally involved tie people to the field so that they are part of a larger profession. Many people really want to use the degree once they earn it. Others want use the degree to work as a librarian for several years at the beginning of their careers so that, if they choose to take a break and work in another field for a while they will have enough experience to come back to libraries if they find they preferred it.

Whether you chose to focus exclusively on library studies classes during your master's degree coursework add other types classes to your degree, you will gain the credentials to work in libraries. At any point along the way you are likely to find that librarians are a helpful bunch. People would not choose librarianship if they did not enjoy helping people. If you want to know more about how libraries work or what different jobs entail, you can ask at your library. It would be an enjoyable change of pace for the librarian at the reference desk, and you might even find someone who would let you shadow them while you are figuring out whether their path is for you.

A number of resources are available to you while you determine whether you want to be a librarian. You can listen in on email discussion lists in order to find out what librarians have to say. You can even use these lists to ask questions. You can read librarians' blogs and wikis, leaving comments and questions there, or you can start your own blog about deciding whether to pursue librarianship. There are free webinars (online seminars), and you can often attend local and regional conferences with student rates. Plenty of resources provide information about the daily work and issues of librarianship and there are many places to get your feet wet before even applying to a program. Your interest and motivation will drive your investigations before you join the field.

Even though the field offers a number of different paths, you do not need to feel like you have to have it all figured out before you get started. A lot of people take the general required classes and maybe a practicum or two before deciding exactly where and in what way they would want to work. Librarianship shares a common set of skills and knowledge across positions and libraries, so if you wait until you are confident about your career choice you will not miss out on anything. A lot of people transition to a different type of library or position once they are in the field, too. Some choose broad jobs when they first start out just to get a variety of experiences and to keep as many doors as possible open further down the road.

If librarianship sounds like it might be right for you, you can sample the many options and paths ahead of you, or you can chose a specific target and get started working towards that goal. You probably have librarians in your community who are willing and able to help you make sense of the field as a whole, as well as a host of people online. You will be part of a field that embraces your background and existing skills, allows you to keep learning, and has a number of professional development opportunities if you have an interest in pursuing them. If it sounds interesting, and like something you could enjoy doing, then you have to figure out the best way to get involved and to get started. We look forward to your joining us!

Appendix 1: Glossary

AASL: American Association of School Librarians; An organization for school librarians and media specialists

ACRL: Association of College and Research Libraries; An organization for librarians at college and research libraries

ADA: Americans with Disabilities Act; libraries' physical and online spaces must comply with this act

ALA: American Library Association; the flagship institution for librarians in North America

ALCTS: Association for Library Collections and Technical Services; An organization for technical services library staff, a division of this organization aims to support preservation librarians

ALSC: Association for Library Service to Children; An organization for librarians that serve children, both school and public librarians

ALTA: Association for Library Trustees & Advocates; An organization for board members, library friends, and other library supporters

Approval plan: A list of materials that the library will always purchase, allows the library to automate the selection process

ARL: Association of Research Libraries; An association of the highest level of research libraries

ASCLA: Association of Specialized and Cooperative Library Agencies

Bibliographic instruction: see *Library instruction*

Blended librarianship: Librarianship that also includes technology and education skills

Blog: A social technology consisting of posts displayed in reverse chronological order

Chat: A synchronous method of communicating online

Content management system: A system that allows users to share content with each other and add content to a website with minimal technical knowledge

Copy cataloging: The act of downloading records from OCLC and modify them before adding them to the catalog

Creative Commons: A copyright license system designed to flexibly handle copyright sharing

CSS: Cascading Style Sheets; see Style sheets

CV: Curriculum Vitae; A longer form resume com-
              mon in academia

Fixed term scheduling: A way of scheduling school
              media centers in which classes come to the li-
              brary on a regular basis.

Flex term scheduling: A way of scheduling school
              media centers in which classes come to the li-
              brary at a specific point of need.

IM: Instant Message; See *Chat*

Institution repository: A digital repository that is de-
              signed to collect the work of a specific institution

Integrated library system: The system that runs a
              bulk of the library's business; technical services,
              the catalog, access services, etc.

Interlibrary loan: A system that allows libraries to
              share materials in order to secure resources for
              their users

JavaScript: A scripting language often used in websites

Library 2.0: A recent movement in librarianship that
              originated as a response to Web 2.0 and has
              evolved to include the physical building and
              real life services

Library instruction: Anytime librarians teach classes
on how to use the library or to do research

LITA: Library and Information Technology Association; an organization for librarians at any library interested in technology issues

LLAMA: Library Leadership and Management
Association; An organization for library
administration and people interested in library
leadership

MLS: Master's degree in library studies; the entry
level requirement for most librarian positions

MARC Record: A type of cataloging record

OCLC: Online Computer Library Center

OPAC: Online Public Access Catalog; the online interface to search the library's collection

Open access: Publication model which does not charge
the readers or the institution for access to
articles

Open source: Code that is available to the public for
use or modification from its original design free
of charge

Outreach: A way of reaching out to the community to
market services

Peer reviewed: A system of publishing in which peers in your field review your work and approve it before it can be published

Periodicals: See *Serials*

PLA: Public Library Association; An organization for public library librarians

Programs: Information sessions or events

Provost: The chief academic officer in a college or university

Public domain: Materials no longer protected under copyright

Roving reference: Reference services offered by a librarian moving throughout the building

RUSA: Reference and User Services Association; An organization for reference librarians and others working in user services

Serials: Publications with recurring issues that are published with no predetermined end date

SLA: Special Libraries Association

Style sheets: A way of streamlining the design of a website; one style can be applied to a number of different pages within a site

Third place: The third place you spend your time, after home and work

Web 2.0: The shift of the Internet towards an environment in which it is easy to contribute content

Weed: Removing selected materials from the collection

Wiki: A website consisting of interlinking pages that are really easy to edit

YALSA: The Young Adult Library Services Association; An organization for librarians working with Young Adults, both in school and public libraries

Appendix 2: Interviews

School Librarianship
Sue Kimmel

What type of library do you work in and what is your job title? What type of work do you do in a typical week?

I work in a small, but challenging elementary school with about 275 students in preschool through fifth grade. I call myself a school librarian but my official title is "media coordinator." On a typical school day we are busy with students returning and checking out books. I have an assistant for a couple of hours a day who facilitates circulation. I have also successfully used student assistants (fourth and fifth graders) for checking books in and out. Assistants and volunteers help with shelving. Every week I meet with at least one grade level to plan units and lessons. I recommend and gather materials for teachers to use and together we plan lessons for the students to come to the library. I may see small groups of students or entire classes depending on the lesson. My lessons integrate library research and literature with content. My daily schedule varies according to what lessons are planned and even my lunch time is flexible. I have hall duty during dismissal and I use this time to connect with students and faculty at the end of the day. I try to learn everyone's name.

What are your favorite parts of your work?

The favorite parts of my job are the people I work with: students, teachers, and administrators. My work touches everyone in the school including outreach to parents and families. I like working with younger children because they are so imaginative, open, and affectionate. As a school librarian, I am considered a teacher and I enjoy being a part of a collegial staff as we collaborate to nego- tiate the meanings of curriculum, learning, and assess- ment. Because I work with the entire school community, I am in a leadership position which allows me to liaison between grade level teams and the administration. I also enjoy getting a chance to work in every discipline: math and science as well as language arts and social studies. I really enjoy the flexibility, continuing education, and in- tellectual challenge of my job.

What is the most challenging aspect of your work?

Probably the most challenging aspect of working in public schools is the rate of change and changing mandates. A new group of kindergarteners enter each year and stu- dents turnover throughout the school year. Every year new teachers join the school and the administration also changes occasionally. New relationships must be negoti- ated as well as budgets, staffing, and use of time. Curricu- lum changes and new initiatives are introduced by local, state, and federal mandates. Professional development is ongoing and often mandated as well. The challenge is to remember the ideals that led me to choose librarianship as a career and to work in the public schools. The stu- dents keep me grounded; I love to see them discover favorite books and authors as well as their enthusiasm for learning. While I am the sole librarian in the building, I find that working with teachers and administrators allows me to grow in my own understanding and leadership abilities.

What piece of advice would you give a student interested in librarianship?

My advice to students interested in librarianship is to stay open. I didn't picture myself in a school library when I went to library school but I have found it to be the most interesting and satisfying place to work. Librarianship is a great career choice because there are so many directions it may take you in. I love the variety in my job.

Academic Libraries
Kim Duckett

What type of library do you work in and what is your job title?

My title is Principal Librarian for Digital Technologies and Learning and I work at North Carolina State University, a large research university. My library is big. We have more than 250 staff—about 115 of them are librarians. My job is a "blended librarian" position and incorporates skills of traditional librarianship with learning technologies and instructional design.

What type of work do you do in a typical week?

My job is diverse. During a typical week I work several hours covering our "Ask Us" virtual reference service, when I answer questions from students via email and instant messaging. I also serve as co-project manager for a big project in our library that is focused on creating sets of library resources for students to help them find information for their course projects. I work with several programmers for this project as well as many other librarians. Additionally, I work a lot with technologies such as learning management systems like Blackboard, wikis, and blogs. I answer questions from faculty and other librarians about these technologies. And like many librarians in large research libraries, I'm on a variety of committees where I collaborate with colleagues to make decisions for our library.

What are your favorite parts of your work?

One aspect of my job that I love is managing projects to development new web-based tools and services for our library users. It's great to start with an idea, work with a variety of colleagues or other stakeholders like students and faculty, and develop a new tool or service that will help people find information more easily from the library's website. I also love to teach students how to use information resources such as article databases, Google Scholar, and the library's catalog. I especially love to teach students about how information gets created and debated in society.

What is the most challenging aspect of your work?

The most challenging aspect of my work is time management. Because I have such an interesting job, there are many great projects that come my way. My library's administration and my colleagues also often turn to me for information or advice pertaining to my particular specialization in the library and this adds to the amount of interesting work I get involved in. As a result, it can be challenging for me to make sure I keep enough time in my schedule for me to work on in-depth projects and balance all I need to do.

What piece of advice would you give a student interested in librarianship?

Take any chances you can to work with librarians and talk to them about their particular interests and areas of expertise. If you can volunteer or get a paid job in a library, you'll be exposed to so much more than appears on the surface. Librarians have jobs that are very different from what people assume they do....and much, much more interesting! In fact, it can be hard for librarians to describe to other people what they actually do. And most librarians love to talk about their work and want to encourage students to consider librarianship. So take any chances you can to dig beneath the surface of librarians' work by talking to them and seek out opportunities to actually become part of the library's work yourself.

Public Libraries
Amy Kearns

What type of library do you work in and what is your job title?

[Before my current position] I worked in an urban public library—my job title is Head of the Reference Department.

What type of work do you do in a typical week?

- Scheduling a staff of four full-timers for the department, including scheduling on and off reference desk time.
- Coaching and managing this staff. We held weekly department meetings and worked on setting and achieving individual goals.
- Assisting patrons with reference questions and computer assistance.
- Ordering books for the reference collection and managing and weeding this collection—ordered also for other collections in the library as needed—also included informational DVDs.
- Covered the homework help computer room once a week - also helped to schedule and manage this room and those covering it.
- Provided training for all library staff on new tech tools, such as wikis, social bookmarking, and databases.
- Conducted tours and introductions of the library to school groups, new users, adult ESL groups, etc.
- Assisted with Young Adult collection development and programming.

- Created and assisted with an adult Conversation Club.
- Managed Interlibrary Loan services.
- Made visits to schools to connect with teachers and students about being a librarian and also about the library.
- Covered other library branches as needed.

What are your favorite parts of your work?

Training and managing staff were some of my personal favorite things—trying to increase the customer service we provided and the level of assistance and service and programs we were able to provide for our public. Also trying to innovate in the library. It was enjoyable and challenging to move the library and staff forward....

What is the most challenging aspect of your work?

Dealing with the different levels and abilities that both staff and the public have when trying to assist them with technology or other needs. There can be such a large difference in ability and comfort when dealing with technology. The approach must be tailored to each person as a result.

Also, in the urban public library it can be challenging to deal with some of the more difficult patrons.

What piece of advice would you give a student interested in librarianship?

There are so many possible types of jobs in the field of librarianship! Follow your own interests and talents and there will be something rewarding and wonderful that you can do with your degree. Working in librarianship for me allows me to have a very rewarding and satisfying career while knowing I am really and truly helping others and making a difference in the world. This was a very important quality that I personally felt I needed to have in my work. Librarianship can give you this.

Special Libraries
Rachel R. Walden

What type of library do you work in and what is your job title?

I work in an academic medical center library and am titled, simply, "librarian." We have medical and nursing schools that we serve, as well as hospital and outpatient clinics.

What type of work do you do in a typical week?

This really varies—my work on any given day might involve looking for articles for physicians to support their patient care decisions, training on the library's resources, more traditional hours on the library's service desks, or work on any number of special projects we're involved in, which may take place in or outside of the library. In my environment, people aren't necessarily roped off into only one type of project or task, so I have a lot of variety and interest in my work.

What are your favorite parts of your work?

Our support of evidence-based medicine in the form of creating summary packets is very interesting—the librarians search the literature, and don't just throw a ton of citations at the doctor—we read, select, and summarize the best and most relevant evidence for the question. This requires a fair bit of background knowledge on medical terminology, study methodology, and so on, but it's always a challenge. That's one example of my favorite aspect—there is always some type of challenge to tackle or something new to do or learn in medical librarianship.

What is the most challenging aspect of your work?

I am always thinking about how we can make sure our community is aware of our services and our skills. We do a lot of work outside the library, and have made terrific strides in that area, but I always worry about that one person who could really use our help but just doesn't know that it's available. I suppose it's also a challenge in terms of keeping up, building my knowledge base, but I see that as a very positive aspect of the work.

What piece of advice would you give a student interested in librarianship?

I would tell a student to get some practical, hands-on experience. I worked in my current library while obtaining my MLIS, and I think that experience both helped me know that I was going into the right field and gave me an understanding of the environment that I wouldn't have if I had simply gotten the degree out of interest with no experience at all. I think that gaining some practical experience will also be a huge help to students as they seek employment.

Also, while they are in their MLIS programs, it's useful to seek out relevant medical librarianship coursework, but also to think about how an individual assignment might reflect that medical interest, and how practicum or independent study opportunities can be adapted to focus on medical librarianship. At the same time, students should not ignore their non-medically-focused elective opportunities. I took a government documents course that turned out to not only be very interesting, but extremely useful for a project that arose just months after graduation.

Access Services Librarian
Mary Chimato

What type of library do you work in and what is your job title?

My title is Head, Access & Delivery Services. The short answer about my work is that I oversee circulation, course reserves, interlibrary loan and document delivery, the microform/media center, stacks maintenance, and the satellite shelving facility. The longer answer is that my work involves all of the public services in the library that are not related to reference or instruction. My department staffs three service desks in the library—a main circulation desk, an express circulation desk, and the desk in the microform/media center. We handle all circulation transactions, which include borrowing/returning items, retrieving items from the stacks, processing patron holds, processing patron financial transactions, and answering any questions that we are asked. We make a lot of referrals to other areas of the libraries. My department is also responsible for processing interlibrary loan and document delivery transactions. ILL staff borrow materials from other libraries for our patrons, and provide materials for patrons at other institutions. They also provide a document delivery service for materials that are housed in our offsite storage facilities. My staff are also responsible for the media and microform collections, as well as the bookstacks.

What type of work do you do in a typical week?

In a typical week I attend a lot of meetings where we discuss projects that are either happening or are coming up. I also deal with any facilities or security issues that may impact my department or the areas that my department oversees. In a typical week my staff shelve books, assist patrons with their ILL requests, check-in new media, facilitate the moving of items from branches to our storage facility, pull materials from the stacks that patrons have placed holds upon, they search for lost or missing items, and they pull materials from the stacks for ILL requests. No day is the same and the work is always changing.

What are your favorite parts of your work and what is the most challenging aspect of your work?

My answer is the same for both of these questions. The most challenging and enjoyable part of my work is the fast pace and constant change of what is happening in the department. We deal with everything and anything and sometimes we have to make up processes or policies on the fly for something new or that has changed. Managing the fast pace and the change can be challenging at times, but it is also a lot of fun.

What piece of advice would you give a student interested in librari-anship?

Try to figure out what type of work you enjoy doing and then look for a position that allows you to do it. Be flexi-ble and roll with the punches. Understand that change is a constant in this profession and if you are someone who does not enjoy change, then this is not the career for you. Taking risks is a good thing and can move you forward. Failure is not a bad thing, and trying out new ideas can be fun and exciting. Do not underestimate the importance of knowing how to get along well and work together with other people. A lot of library work is team-based and what you do often has an impact on another person or department. Most of our work does not exist in a vacuum.

Reference Librarian
Ellie Collier

What type of library do you work in and what is your job title?

Academic (Community College) Reference Librarian/Assistant Professor

What type of work do you do in a typical week?

I would say there's no such thing as a typical week. My work flows with the school year, so in the beginning of the Fall we're getting ready for the classes that are starting up and selecting books because our budget has just replenished. By mid Fall we're really digging into projects as well as doing more instruction as teachers are bringing their classes in to learn how to do research for their upcoming papers. By the end of Fall we try to have at least half of our orders for the year in. Spring has a lot of the same flow, with May being the deadline for ordering books. Those of us that don't take the summer off spend it weeding and catching up on projects.

During a week there's a little bit of everything—faculty meetings, committee meetings, selecting books, instruction, reference desk hours, creating tutorials, professional reading, etc....

What are your favorite parts of your work?

I really love collection development—learning about new subject areas and selecting materials.

What is the most challenging aspect of your work?

Learning how much you can cover in half-hour long information sessions.

Educational Technology Librarian
Melissa Rethlefsen

What type of library do you work in and what is your job title?

I work in a small medical school library (2 full time staff) that is part of a larger academic health center library system. My job title is Education Technology Librarian.

What type of work do you do in a typical week?

Because only I and one other person work full time in my library, I wind up doing a huge variety of types of work. One of my main responsibilities is management, from approving time cards to managing construction projects to hiring student staff. I choose what books, journals, and other materials are added to my library's collections; help design and maintain the library's web site; perform literature searches; help medical students with reference questions or learning how to use databases; and teach library sections of the medical school curriculum. I also do the basic stuff like check out books. I participate in the wider Mayo Clinic Libraries system, where I develop and teach classes, serve on technology and management committees, and work at the main library's reference desk. In addition, I work on a lot of research projects with Clinic staff and other library staff and participate in associations like the Medical Library Association.

What are your favorite parts of your work?

My absolute favorite part is working with the medical students and getting to know them over the four years they are here. I also really enjoy teaching, picking the materials for the collection, and anything to do with technology (e.g., web design).

What is the most challenging aspect of your work?

The most challenging part of what I do is probably just navigating the politics of a large institution.

What piece of advice would you give a student interested in librarianship?

Get involved with library associations right away, whether your local association or a national association. Participate as much as you can—you'll meet a lot of mentors and colleagues who will be there for you the rest of your career, and you'll see a world outside of your library.

E-Resources Librarian
Courtney Stephens

What type of library do you work in and what is your job title?

I work in a small, private university library. My job title is Electronic and Educational Resources Librarian.

What type of work do you do in a typical week?

In a typical week, I lead instruction sessions for our first
year classes, meet with the departments I am a liaison to,
spend some time on the reference desk, answer emails,
renew database subscriptions, troubleshoot the proxy
server, troubleshoot our PC access software, updating our
website, and anything else that is needed.

What are your favorite parts of your work?

My favorite parts of my work are very different. I enjoy
working with students, at the reference desk and during
instruction sessions. I also enjoy making sure the students,
faculty and staff can access our resources and website.

What is the most challenging aspect of your work?

The most challenging aspect of my work is probably talking to and negotiating with vendors. I think this is the part
that I am most uncomfortable with, and I would like to
know more about effective negotiation strategies.

*What piece of advice would you give a student interested in librari-
anship?*

Work in a library. Before you go to library school, or
while you're there, you should work in a library. You
should also look at yourself and see if you are a truly curious person who loves to learn new things. Librarianship
today is not just about the theories you learn in library
school. It's about helping people adapt to the "informa-

tion age" and teaching them to handle the new forms of
information that we are all inundated with.

Cataloger Librarian
Kathleen Burlingame

What type of library do you work in and what is your job title?

I work in a rare books and manuscripts library that is part
of a larger institution with a performance theater and exhibition space. In addition to textual materials, our collection contains visual art and realia. I am a Manuscript
Cataloger working with a team of three other catalogers
on a three year grant funded project.

What type of work do you do in a typical week?

My typical work week mainly consists of recon cataloguing, original cataloguing, and authority work. Consequently, I spend a lot of time on the computer and consulting original materials in the vault. These documents
include personal letters, diaries, commonplace books, po-
etical miscellanies, musical manuscripts, political writings,
account books, warrants, and deeds. I also attend meetings with my colleagues to establish local practices which
are then added to an online wiki. Cataloguing standards
and technologies are constantly evolving and working
with rare materials requires additional specialized knowledge, so education is ongoing. Consequently, my work
week will often involve training sessions in, for example,
NACO contribution or paleography. In addition, our patrons (whom we call "readers") give brown bag talks

which I am encouraged to attend. The library will often provide paid leave and funding for trips to relevant conferences and classes at Rare Book School. Opportunities for work beyond my day to day duties are available as well. For example, I am currently helping to curate a collaborative staff exhibition.

What are your favorite parts of your work?

I enjoy having privileged access to a world-renowned collection of books and manuscripts. I am constantly amazed that I am able to hold these magnificent objects and feel such a tangible connection to the past. In addition, I thoroughly appreciate working with people who are incredible intelligent, interesting, and dedicated to their profession. The work is very collaborative and we are constantly sharing our enthusiasm for the materials. It is also comforting to know that my employer is concerned with my professional development and encourages this by providing a generous leave policy and funds for training and travel to conferences. Ultimately though, my greatest satisfaction comes from knowing that what I'm doing will serve the greater academic and artistic community by providing better access to these materials. Working in a collegial environment where academic scholarship and creativity is championed via free access to information is an endless source of joy for me.

What is the most challenging aspect of your work?

Cataloguing involves a large amount of mental stamina. There is always more work to be done and the quality and depth of cataloguing must constantly be weighed with the quantity of materials that needs to be processed. Catalogers must also have a high tolerance for ambiguity…no standard is set in stone since there are always exceptions to the rules. There is a certain degree of subjective judgment that must go into almost every catalog description which must also be balanced with a need for consistency. Flexibility is key. This balancing act may be challenging, but it also makes the work creative, highly intellectual, collaborative, and exciting.

What piece of advice would you give a student interested in librarianship?

Do it for the right reasons. In other words, become a librarian because you feel passionately attracted to the work and people involved (both patrons and colleagues). There really isn't any fame or fortune in librarianship…the reward is in the work itself and the satisfaction of knowing that you are providing a great service to the work of others.

While it may be useful to gain experience in a paraprofessional capacity before heading to library school, I believe it is also useful to have knowledge of the world outside of libraries as well. My prior career in corporate publishing has not only given me great insight into the process of textual production, but has also allowed me to appreciate the benefits of working in an environment where intellectual integrity and collaborative efforts are valued over monetary profit and personal gain. Ultimately, libraries do not exist in a vacuum, but rather are cultural, social, and political nexuses. Staying actively involved in communities beyond a narrowly defined conception of "the profession" keeps you relevant and savvy.

Special Collections Librarian
Audra Eagle

What type of library do you work in and what is your job title?

I work in a local history and genealogy department of an urban public library. My job title is Librarian.

What type of work do you do in a typical week?

In a typical week I work 10-15 hours at the local history and genealogy reference desk answering questions about family history, state laws, as well as the history and culture of our city and county. I usually meet with the head of my department or another administrator to discuss grants or special collections projects such as processing a newly acquired genealogical manuscript or the potential for digitization for some of our early photographs. One day, I might find myself planning our next genealogy program, such as a workshop about doing genealogy online, or writing a grant to preserve our collections; the next day, I am working with a donor to bring in a new collection or buying books on the history of Africa for the entire library system.

What are your favorite parts of your work?

Getting to work with something and someone new every day is the best part about being a special collections li-

brarian. While I get to work with the public at the reference desk, I also get to use my training as an archivist to
arrange, describe, and preserve rare books, manuscripts,
photographic materials, audiovisual materials, maps, and
other items that need special care. Being able to make
these materials available for researchers, genealogists, and
historians is what makes my job worthwhile.

What is the most challenging aspect of your work?

Special collections librarianship is all about advocacy.
There is a great deal of public misconception or igno-
rance of special collections and the amount of access
permitted. Often, budgetary constraints can prevent
proper cataloging or digitization of special materials in
your library. You have to learn to extol the virtues of
keeping rare, valuable, and local materials preserved, se-
cured, and accessible to administrators and the public
alike.

*What piece of advice would you give a student interested in librari-
anship?*

Remember to try everything at least once. If there is an
area in which you are interested, get in touch with someone in that field or try to get an internship there. Networking is the bread and butter of librarianship. While
you are in school, take advantage of your status and
watch doors open up before you. Make your own business
cards as a student and hand them out freely. It is much
harder to get an informational interview or an internship
after you have graduated! Your connections will prove

invaluable when it comes time to apply for library school and especially so when you begin to look for a job.

Digital Projects Librarian
Cat McDowell

What type of library do you work in and what is your job title?

Academic research library, Digital Projects Coordinator.

What type of work do you do in a typical week?

Evaluate potential new projects; perform quality control on imaging and image descriptions; create project workflows, standards, templates, and policies, and evaluate progress; basic HTML, XML, or ASP coding; create database specifications; research descriptive and other standards

What are your favorite parts of your work?

I love making archival materials accessible to the entire world, and seeing them used. I love the combination, however ironic, of cutting-edge, emerging technologies and centuries-old archival material. And I love enhancing order and standardization through the digitization process.

What is the most challenging aspect of your work?

The technology itself is often challenging for me, and that is probably often the case; the nature of digitization is that it usually requires a broad set of skills which no one person can be an expert in, especially those of us with library and not IT degrees. So thankfully, when I need help on an aspect of a project, I know I can call on my server administrator, database administrator, web developer, application coder, or anyone else with more specific IT skills in our library to help out!

What piece of advice would you give a student interested in librarianship?

1) I think ever-increasingly, libraries are about information access and knowledge management—and what that means is ever-changing! So if you aren't comfortable with technology or change, librarianship may not be the career for you. Conversely, if you've thought that librarians just sit at a desk reading books all day, you should be aware that it can be a cutting-edge, envelope-pushing career perfect for those who love innovation.

2) If you know specifically what aspect of librarianship you are interested in, choose a library school that has a specialized curriculum track for that.

3) Find a student job in the library, or volunteer if you have to! The best way to know if you'll like something is to do it, and on-the-job training is invaluable as a learning experience AND as a résumé builder!

Technology Librarian
Cliff Landis

What type of library do you work in and what is your job title?

I'm the Technology Librarian at Valdosta State University. The title is intentionally ambiguous so that I can work on any technology-related initiatives that need to be done.

What type of work do you do in a typical week?

I work on initiatives related to technology across the library. I usually have my hand in several projects at once. I might work on building and revising databases, running research studies (usability, user satisfaction, etc.), update blogs and social network profiles, run reports on the library's website, etc. I also work on the reference desk and teach library instruction sessions and semester-long courses.

What are your favorite parts of your work?

Most of my initiatives are very different from each other, allowing me to do lots of different things. That variety is a perk for me. Also, I make sure that my projects (even the ongoing ones) have clear beginnings and endings, so that I can have clear goals. This is also important to me.

What is the most challenging aspect of your work?

I have a tendency to over-volunteer, and there is always more work that needs to be done (especially related to technology!). I have to be careful of taking on too much, and make sure that I don't make it my personal mission to fix every problem by myself. My coworkers are always great at helping me prioritize, especially when there are lots of problems waiting for solutions.

What piece of advice would you give a student interested in librarianship?

First, love change. If you can't deal with change (especially technological change) don't become a librarian. Second, get an internship. I learned a lot in library school, but it was no substitute for working in a library. Third, think of the users. Libraries are not built for librarians; they are built for library users. Remember that when it's decision-making time.

Index

About the Author

Lauren Pressley is the Instructional Design Librarian at Wake Forest University. She has worked in libraries since 2003, and earned her MLIS from the University of North Carolina-Greensboro in 2007. She is active in the American Library Association, Library and Information Technology Association, and the Association of College and Research Libraries and she regularly presents and writes on issues relating to education and technology in libraries. She was a member of the 2008 ALA Emerging Leaders class and was named a *Library Journal* Mover & Shaker in 2009. Her website is http://laurenpressley.com.

CPSIA information can be obtained at www.ICGtesting.com
Printed in the USA
BVOW04s0033230914

367866BV00022B/364/P